Nigel Pearce

Notes

from

the

symposium

Nigel Pearce

Nigel Pearce

Published by
Chipmunkapublishing
United Kingdom

http://www.chipmunkapublishing.com

Copyright © 2018 Nigel Pearce

ISBN   978-1-78382-452-6

Nigel Pearce

Nigel has lived a life of extremes: on the streets, in squats, enforced medication and E.C.T by the age of sixteen. He escaped his addictions, long, long ago and now lives where he had sought sanctuary as a child: a world of books, writing and ideas. This is his eleventh book with Chipmunkapublishing and his first written solely from the academy. He has gained two bachelor's degrees both at 2/1, one is in creative writing, and he has recently added a *Postgraduate Diploma in Humanities* to these. He awaits the results of his M.A. English. All studied at The Open University.

He lives with mental illness which imposes many limitations on him. Yet his intellect and creativity are free although disciplined as they must be in order to write both prose and poetry.

Nigel Pearce

Nigel Pearce

Contents.

Nigel Pearce

Nigel Pearce

Chartist poetics: an echo of Romanticism or a nascent proletarian literature?

Abstract:

This dissertation is unashamedly about labouring-class poetry. However, the journey of research took me to texts and ideas which I had not encountered previously. Essentially, it examines the tensions between a progressive, yet mainly elite Romanticism and the autodidactic labouring-class poetry which arose as a consequence of the struggles around the Six-Point Charter for the vote [for men] and then the Leftist endeavours for 'the charter and something more' which gained momentum after the revolutions in continental Europe and the Irish insurgency of the same year, 1848. My two major Chartist poets are Thomas Cooper and Ernest Jones. Chapter One examines the recent scholarship of Anne Janowitz and Mike Sanders as a foundation for my investigation and I use Wordsworth as a 'barometer' of the epoch. Chapter Two and I look at some Chartist broadsheets and journals and recognize a Leftward drift. These two chapters form the spine of my dissertation. Chapter Three examines the 'Left Turn' of 1848. My conclusion considers questions of proletarian aesthetics in and beyond Chartism including those of the early avant-garde in the USSR until the imposition of Socialist Realism as a doctrine at the Writers Congress in 1934. This counter-revolutionary blow is explained, and the future of labouring-class poetry is seen to exist in the literary praxis I located in Britain during the period of Chartism and the experimental 'laboratories' advocated by people like Alexander Bogdanov.

Nigel Pearce

Nigel Pearce

Contents.

Introduction: A world to win?

Chapter One: The Romantic experience in relation to the Chartist poetic.

Chapter Two: Contrasting Chartist publications and perspectives on poetry.

Chapter Three: 1848, the 'left turn' and the poetry of class struggle.

Conclusion: On aesthetics, experiments and futures

Nigel Pearce

Introduction: a world to win?

The rationale and relationship of my dissertation to A815 was that the former had kindled an interest in the relationship between Lord Byron and John Clare. I wanted to explore what happened when the poor became organized in the light of Romanticism. Discovering the autodidactic tradition of the Chartists was important. Here were a collectivity of poor poets who did not lose their sanity but actively contested both poetically and politically the dominant literary terrain. The problem my dissertation's title sets up to be solved is simply this. To what extent was the flowering of British labouring-class poetry during the period of Chartism, 1836-52, to be seen to have evolved and differentiated itself from Romanticism and the other dominant mode of poetry of the epoch, the dramatic monologue? Did this poetry become an autonomous class literature? Indeed, is the latter possible under the conditions of capitalism? Also, I shall have to provide an explanatory framework to show how and why poetry was a dominant form in the proletariat while it was becoming marginalized in the mainstream. The novel would become the favoured reading of the middle- classes. Nevertheless, some Chartist prose was written, but does not stand reasonable comparison with the sustained and diverse body of Chartist poetry.[1] The poetry was, with few exceptions, written by working men and women who would have had little or no access to the rules and norms of 'form' other than from assimilating them through what they had read or heard rather than through formal education. I shall understand the solution
to my conundrum will lie in a qualitatively different society, one not based on commodification.

Thus, my contention is that it was in the form and the material conditions of its composition which made Chartist poetics counter-hegemonic. The puzzle is complicated once the veil of ideology is removed:

The ideas of the ruling class are in every epoch the ruling ideas, i.e. the class which is the ruling material force of society, is at the same time its ruling intellectual force. The class which has the means of material production at its disposal, has control at the same time over the means of mental production, so that thereby, generally speaking, the ideas of those who lack the means of mental production are subject to it. The ruling ideas are nothing more than the ideal expression of the dominant material relationships...[2]

Hence, we understand that behind the veil of material inequality lay one of mental dissimilarity. By challenging that Chartism contested the very heart of bourgeois culture. Indeed, for their endeavour to succeed they would have needed to put a stake through it. Marx twice intended to write a treatise on aesthetics but on both occasions

---

[1] *The Literature of Struggle: An Anthology of Chartist Fiction* [ed] Haywood, Ian (London, Routledge, 1995).
[2] Marx, Karl & Engels Frederick *The German Ideology* (London, Lawrence & Wishart, 1982) p, 62.

failed to complete it. Hence the breadth of Marxist aesthetics. My position is that the two analytical instruments of the Marxist project, historical materialism and dialectical materialism, must provide the methodology and illuminate the social circumstance of any attempt to arrive at a meaningful understanding of the relationship between class and literature. In a late letter Engels hinted that the Formalist project is not a blind alley as Plekhanov argued. The latter is the father of a crude Marxist 'Reflectionism in matters of society and literature. Rather Engels, by arguing as (Hemingway, 2005, p.3) makes clear 'different spheres of intellectual production have what Engels call 'inherent relative independence.' [3]

Nevertheless, given these caveats we can understand that Chartist writers were connected to a mass movement which Lenin called: 'the first genuinely mass revolutionary movement', 'the word but one before Marxism' [4]. *That the unique and cross-generic nature of the original primary material was a 'counter-hegemonic' questioning of an emerging and multifaceted bourgeois narrative.*

I will focus on Thomas Cooper and Ernest Jones who had very different social and ideological trajectories within Chartism, both wrote voluminously. Also, they were incarcerated for being leaders of Chartism, Thomas Cooper in 1842 and Ernest Jones in 1848, show the reasons for the failure of Chartism and, therefore a counter- hegemonic British labouring-class poetic, and argue that for proletarian writers to thrive a society based on 'use-value' rather than 'exchange value' is necessary. Where the masses have control of the material 'means of production'. The work of William Morris on aesthetics is significant but, I argue flawed. I also venture that the ideas of Boris Arvatov and some around the short-lived Soviet avant-garde like Bogdanov who sought to create a 'laboratory for pure proletarian ideology' [5] *in which to experiment with the emancipated literary form. Although problematic, Lenin criticized Prolecult which was a Left art movement aiming at the creation of a new art and literature, one which was collectivised because the proletariat is a collectivity of individual voices in 1920.* [6] *I will argue in the conclusion that this represented a cauldron of ideas about proletarian poetics as yet to be superseded. I find support in perceiving a link between the Chartists and the October Revolution in the early work of Reg Groves.* [7] *Also later with the investigations of Mark Krantz.* [8]

Thomas Cooper was an autodidact, embraced 'physical force Chartism', was imprisoned for his role in the General Strike of 1842, wrote the Purgatory of

---

[3] Marx and Engels, Selected correspondence (Moscow, Foreign Languages Press, 1955) p. 503

[4] Lenin V.I. *Collected Works* Vol 30 (Moscow, Progress Publishers,1965) p, 492.

[5] Eagleton, Terry *Marxism and Literary Criticism* (London, Routledge Classics 2008), p, 35.

[6] *Russia Art of the Avant-Garde* [ed] Bowlt, John E. (London, Thames & Hudson, 2017) p. 177.

[7] Groves, Reg *But we shall rise again: A narrative history of Chartism* (London, Secker and Warburg, 1938)

[8] Krantz, Mark *The 1842 General Strike* (London, Bookmarks,2014).

Suicides: A Prison-Rhyme in 922 Spenserian stanzas, became a 'moral force Chartist' remaining sceptical of Christianity, and eventually became an itinerant Baptist preacher denying Darwinism on biblical grounds. We can see how the laws of Historical Materialism were working here i.e. a material base for the superstructure of ideas. I will elaborate further on this, but it will be made clear that is not a mechanistic relationship if only because the dialectic is buried in history, obscured by the veil of ideology, creating its opposite. The Chartist movement was not a homogeneous one. It was fraught with divisions and factions.

This 'hidden history' is again stimulating interest in academia with new publications like Anne Janowitz *Lyric and Labour in the Romantic Tradition* (1998), Mike Sanders *The Poetry of Chartism: Aesthetics, Politics, History* (2009), *Class and the Canon: Constructing Labouring Class Poetry and Poetics* (ed) Kirstie Blair and Mina Gorji (2013), and Margaret A. Loose *The Chartist Imaginary: Literary Forms in Working-Class Political Theory and Debate* (2014).[9]

I would like to stress that Chartist poetry in its first generation was largely, when committed to paper, published in a nationwide network of periodicals, journals and broadsheets. This analysis will examine a number across a socio-cultural spectrum during the period 1836-52 and refer to a second generation which were published in book form in the later nineteenth-century to the early twentieth century. The book history will be explored as my dissertation is developed. It is important to recognize that Chartist poetics was the pinnacle of a radical autodidactic culture in Britain. It was multisource, but hunger was significant as by 'the hungry-forties' a stratum of the poor was facing starvation. I note that Thomas Frost who was a utopian socialist or Owenite but would not cross the line to fully fledged communist but was a Chartist, remembered:

> *Webecame acquainted that evening, and, in the course of many subsequent years, I passed an agreeable half-hour in the shoemaker's garret, talking by turns of politics and poetry.*[10]

As my research has unfolded it became evident that this was by no means an unusual experience as a politicized working-class became increasingly interested in articulating themselves in poetic terms. It was a movement that would move leftwards.

My variant of Marxist methodology is derived from György Lukács' study into the nature of Marxist dialectics. I required a rigorous theory for this investigation into Chartist poetics:

> *Let us assume for the sake of argument that recent research had disproved once and for all every one of Marx's individual theses... Orthodox Marxism, therefore, does not imply the uncritical acceptance of*

---

[9] Charlton, John *The Chartists: The First National Workers' Movement* (London: Pluto Press, 1997), p. 64

[10] Frost, Thomas *Forty Years' Recollections: Literary and Political* (London: S. Low, Marston, Searle, and Rivington, 1880) p, 34.

the results of Marx's investigations. It is not the 'belief' in this or that thesis, nor the exegesis of a 'sacred' book. On the contrary, orthodoxy refers exclusively to method.[11]

Therefore, I am interested in Dialectical Materialism as a method. Firstly, the transformation from a quantitative to a qualitative condition, thus producing a new state and secondly Interdependent material opposites which are by nature antagonistic, finally 'the negation of the negation' which creates a new thesis afresh with elements of the old but also completely new material. I will delineate two core concepts: 1) the Marxist dialectic [Karl Marx never used the term dialectical materialism]. Here is Engels famous summary in Dialectics of Nature: II. Dialectics

> *(The general nature of dialectics to be developed as the science of interconnections, in contrast to metaphysics.)*
>
> *It is, therefore, from the history of nature and human society that the laws of dialectics are abstracted. For they are nothing but the most general laws of these two aspects of historical development, as well as of thought itself. And indeed, they can be reduced in the main to three:*
> *The law of the transformation of quantity into quality and vice versa; The law of the interpenetration of opposites;*
> *The law of the negation of the negation.*
> *All three are developed by Hegel in his idealist fashion as mere laws of thought... The mistake... is made out to be arranged in accordance witha system of thought which itself is only the product of a definite stage of evolution of human thought. If we turn the thinground...it isclear as noonday.[12]*

Hence, we can comprehend not an abstract or Idealist dialectic but rather one grounded in material reality. Its twin, Historical Materialism, eloquently described by Karl Marx:

> *the first premise of all human history is, of course, the existence of living human individuals. Thus, the first fact to be established is the physical organisation of these individuals and their consequent relation to the rest of nature... The writing of history must always set out from these natural bases and their modification in the course of history through the action of men...[13]*

A number of Marxist theoreticians and others will provide a structure of secondary scholarship. I will examine contemporary scholars of my subject with a special interest in the work of Janowitz (1998) and Sanders (2008). My argument is not that Chartist

---

[11] Lukacs, Georg *History & Class Consciousness: Studies in Marxist Dialectics* (Pontypool, The Merlin Press 2010) p.1

[12] Engels, Frederick *Dialectics of Nature* (Moscow, Progress Publishers, 1976) P. 62-3

[13] Marx and Engels (1982). p.42.

literature was superior or inferior to the bourgeois writers of the time. Rather they were the products of dialectically opposed classes cast in different objective material conditions. Thus, the poetry would be different. I shall, however, suggest that although there was a continuity with Romantic poetry especially during early Chartism with publications like The Chartist Circular which I will reflect upon in the second chapter. This diminished with the bitter General Strike of 1842 and proletarian poetry took a new turn towards didactic realism. We will then understand a leftwards move in Chartism inspired, largely, by the revolutions on continental Europe of 1848. The Programme around this tendency was simply called 'the Charter and something more.' I will illustrate a continuity of Marxist involvement in the form of poetry, publishing and politics from 1843 with the entry of Frederick Engels and continuing into the First, Second, Third and Fourth Internationals [with its splintering] in Britain through to the present day. As Bertolt Brecht suggested 'art is not a mirror to reflect reality, but a hammer to change it'[14]. Indeed, what other use would a proletarian have of it as they are the 'universal class':

> *...a class with radical chains, which cannot emancipate itself without emancipating itself from all other spheres of society and thereby emancipating all other spheres of society, which, in a word, is the complete loss of man and hence can win itself only through the complete rewinning of man[15]*

The class who must because of historical necessity create communism.

---

[14] Brecht, Bertolt in Paulo Freire: A Critical Encounter (1993) by Peter McLaren and Peter Leonard, p. 80."

[15] Marx and Engels, *Collected Works, iii, p. 186, 50 vols published or in preparation* (London, 1975-).

Nigel Pearce

Chapter One.

The Romantic Experience in relation to the Chartist poetic.

This chapter will examine some of the abstractions that lie behind the modern debates around the relationship of Romantic poetry to a working-class Chartist poetics. To arrive at an understanding, we need to examine the most current thinkers and then place them in a narrative of literary theory. This will be the main purpose of this chapter; theorizing and positioning. Firstly, Mike Sanders in his recent exploration of Chartism argues: 'Indeed, it is necessary to return to the work of this neglected 1930's critic, Christopher Caudwell, to begin to comprehend the political effect of poetry'[16]. Sanders quotes Caudwell: 'a poem's content is not just emotion, it is organized emotion, an organized emotional attitude to a piece of external reality.'[17] I continue along a similar line as Mike Sanders in perceiving cogency in some of the positions of Christopher Caudwell:

> *[The] contradiction between individual man or natural man, and associated or civilized man, is what makes poetry necessary, and gives it its meaning and its truth. Poetry is a production or economic activity of man. To separate it from its foundation makes its development impossible to understand.[18]*

We understand that for Christopher Caudwell poetry was as essential to humanity as 'labour'. It was an aspect of what Karl Marx had called our essence or 'species-being.'. Although I recognize the problematic nature of the association between the cultural superstructure with the economic base. Louis Althusser in Lenin on Philosophy and other Essays is useful here when he claimed art can illuminate aspects of the everyday 'sensuous activity' (Marx) of man in the material world. He used the example of Alexander Solzhenitsyn to illustrate the nature of the 'cult of personality' in Stalinist Russia. However, he believed only scientific knowledge can provide the capacity to understand it (Althusser, 2010 pp.153-155). He argued: Art 'in the language of Spinoza it puts the conclusions before the premises.' (Althusser,2010 p. 153). Therefore, Althusser argued art did not follow the laws of formal logic.

Secondly, Anne Janowitz (1998) in her significant and contemporaneous study argued that a dialectic of 'Romantic lyricism' and a 'collective embodied experience of plebeian verse' found fulfilment in the writing of William Morris.[19] She seeks to create a dialectic between the solitary voice associated with Romanticism and the concomitant collective voice of the people. Anne Janowitz understands that there are two component parts in the development from Romantic to Chartist poetry and beyond, a dialectic. The two-component parts are firstly a position which relies on the

---

[16] Sanders, Mike *The Poetry of Chartism: Aesthetics, Politics, History* (Cambridge, Cambridge University Press, 2009). Kindle, 439.
[17] Caudwell, Christopher, *Illusion and Reality* (Lawrence & Wishart, 1973 [1937], p 34-40.
[18] Caudwell, Christopher *Culture as Politics* (Pluto, London, 2018). p 79
[19] Janowitz, Anne *Lyric and Labour in the Romantic tradition*, (Cambridge, Cambridge University Press, (1998), p.7

rejection of theoreticians like John Stuart Mill's definition of Romanticism as a self-sufficient 'lyric' in 1833. Anne Janowitz quotes him: 'feeling confessing itself, in moments of solitude'.[20] She rebuffs in a similar vein, Harold Bloom: 'the sovereignty of the solitary soul... the deep self, our ultimate inwardness.'[21] She argued that both those critics have contributed to the dominant discourse which has shaped Romantic poetry and does indeed constitute a view of the 'Lyric-I' by which she meant the concept of Romantic poet as a solitary voice. We understand Anne Janowitz maintained this position in her argument to provide the thesis to be contradicted by her antithesis, the second component part. This is a 'transpersonal Lyric':

> *This is a lyricism of sociality, of transpersonality rather than transcendence, of achieving connections, and one which, embodying a poetic structure of argument between individualism and communitarianism is both an imagined site for the self-development and imagined instantiation of selves. So, the study aims to understand the position of a communitarian lyric in the tradition of romanticism.'[22]*

Janowitz states she will give priority to this communitarian aspect of Romanticism. However, although this sounds persuasive, exactly how does one achieve the conditions where the Chartist poets Thomas Cooper and Ernest Jones, who she foregrounds, would have been able to create a collective proletarian poetic. As opposed to one which disintegrated with the failure of the Chartist movement to achieve the demands of Left Chartism's 'the Charter and something more.' Her weakness is that her research fails to explore the momentous events for international proletarian literature of the October Revolution. So, she depends on Anglo-Communism rather than proletarian internationalism in the last instance. Although Janowitz alludes to the Chartist mass movement as a precursor to the Paris Commune [23]. I reiterate my position is that the masses must hold State power in order to facilitate the triumph of their poetics. The highest point of labouring- class poetics occurred before the Stalinist counter- revolution in the USSR i.e. between 1917-29 and its defeat was solidified at the Writers Congress in 1934 with the imposition of Socialist Realism.

Nevertheless, her work is important to the first chapter of this dissertation because she correctly illustrates that E. P Thompson was flawed when he argued that William Blake was the last poet who threaded together the discourses of artisan radicalism and romanticism.[24] However because she understands Romanticism and Chartist poetry as

---

[20] Mill, John Stuart. "Thoughts on Poetry and Its Varieties." *The Crayon*, vol. 7, no. 4, 1860, pp. 93–97. ww.jstor.org/stable/25528035. Cambridge University Press, (1998), p.7

[21] Janowitz (1998) pp.7-8

[22] Janowitz (1998), p.8.

[23] See Janowitz, Anne (2008) pp228-230 for a discussion of British socialists and the Commune.

[24] See Thompson, E.P, The Making of the English Working Classes (Harmondsworth, Penguin, 1965), p915

'at home in both cultures' we thus differ on the potential for and on the nature of proletarian poetry. Janowitz remains a Morrisist 'Pilgrim of Hope'. So, my discontent with Janowitz's material is that she finds the fruition of proletarian poetic in William Morris and beyond that although only in writing like that around C.N.D. provided glimmers of hope. Again, paradoxically, she argues W. H. Auden's 'Spain' 'was his greatest poem in the communitarian tradition of Romanticism.' (Janowitz, 1998, p. 234). She unfortunately drifts into the position, of to use Boris Arvatov comment on Morris, that of 'a petty-bourgeois socialist.', one caught between the two great contending classes of capitalism.

In order to provide a provisional framework for this debate I will examine Ernest Jones poem The Factory Town from three perspectives: 1) my reading, 2) Janowitz's and, 3) Margret A. Loose's.

The Factory Town.

The night had sunk along the city,
　It was a bleak and cheerless
hour; The wild-winds sung their
solemn ditty
　To cold, grey wall and blackened tower.

The factories gave forth lurid fires
　From pent-up hells within their
breast; Even Ætna's burning wrath
expires,
　But man's volcanoes never rest.

Women, children, men were in,
　Locked in dungeons close and
black, Round the wheel, the modern
rack!

E'en the very stars seemed
　troubled With the mingled fume
　and roar;
The city like a cauldron bubbled, [25]

Ernest Jones employed a ballad form for The Factory Town and Janowitz speculates that because of its length the poem was sung. I agree as the tradition of the street balladeers were common at this time and of course hymn singing in the dissenting tradition. This couplet is Ernest Jones at his best. It is not tendentious

---

[25] Ernest Jones *The Labourer.*

writing, but he is employing poetry to not only agitate but raise-consciousness about the question of urbanization, the industrial revolution and the emergence of an industrial proletariat:

> The wild-winds sung their solemn
> ditty To cold, grey wall and
> blackenedtower.

The addressee hears the 'wild winds' with both alliteration and assonance [tools employed to some effect by Jones.] They in fact 'sing' a 'solemn ditty. Then he uses enjambment to suddenly increase the pace and then bring to an abrupt halt with a caesura followed by hitting a wall with the harsh 'b' of blackened tower. Anne Janowitz calls this poem: 'One of Jones 'most striking in The Labourer.' (Janowitz, 1998, p181). Here her reading is sound and persuasive about 'double alienation'. 'The labourers labour is separated from him and reified from him and reified into the made products. And then again as he himself is reified and deprived of his self-identity' (Janowitz, 1998 pp181-183). Here she is relying, correctly in my view, on the young Marx. A method I also use in this dissertation.

> Yet the master proudly shows
> To foreign strangers factory scenes:
> 'These are the men – and engines these
>
> —
>
> 'I see nothing but machines!'* [26]

Margret A. Loose's reading has merit. She takes the 'wild winds' I alluded to and contrasts them with 'spitting seas' [L 2-3, 86] and perceives them as metaphors 'for the coming war between workers and masters' (Loose, A. Margaret, 2014, p. 26). Although, I would argue it is not as integrated into the theoretical issues of the day as Janowitz's.

I argue that Wordsworth's early poetry had its foundation in the collapse of community which Wordsworth laments in his letter January 4th, 1804 to Charles Fox in which he sent the 2nd edition of Lyrical Ballads and made special reference to 'The Brothers' and 'Michael'. Both examples of a culture in decline as the industrial revolution transformed Britain [27]. Romanticism could be understood as having gestated in a political tradition which achieved its highest point in France with a revolution which would shake the continent in 1789. Jean-Jacques Rousseau had claimed in The Social Contract (1762): 'Man is born free, and everywhere he lives in chains.' [28] It is often presumed that in Britain the ramifications of this politico-cultural tidal wave was limited to a group of emerging bourgeoisie or disaffected members of the aristocracy such as William Wordsworth and Lord Byron respectively. Artists, in particular poets,

---

[26] Janowitz (1998) p, 182.

[27] Wordsworth, William *Letters of William Wordsworth: a new selection* [ed] Alan G. Hill. (Oxford, Oxford University Press, 1984) pp. 40-45.

[28] Rousseau, Jean-Jacques. *On the Social Contract* (New York, Dover Thrift Editions, 2016) p. 1.

and intellectuals would have commented on these momentous events like Edmund Burke. But what of the mass of people who created history. Were they silent? Until recently the 'big six' had dominated the discourse: William Blake, William Wordsworth, Samuel-Taylor Coleridge, John Keats, Percy Bysshe Shelley and Lord Byron. Because of the scholarship which originated in the work of Raymond Williams which matured into Cultural Materialism and contemporary studies like Duncan Wu Romanticism (1994) followed by Duncan Wu Romantic Women Poets (1997) and the terrain had been broadened. However, it was not until the publication of John Goodridge [Ed] Nineteenth-Century English Labouring Poets in Three Volumes, (2006) that scholars had a substantial pool of working-class poetry which did not originate in the previous USSR (Kovalev, 1956). As I shall illustrate in the next chapter (Kovalev, 1956) had established an early orthodoxy in the field of Chartist literature.

I will employ William Wordsworth in this chapter as a barometer of the epoch. Largely because he lived through the entirety of it unlike any of the other major poets from the ruling elite. Anne Janowitz understands his work over time as 'Jacobinism-in-recoil' (Janowitz 2008, p. 40) which is a phrase she borrowed from E.P. Thompson to describe Wordsworth's apparent retreat from the revolutionary cause. He had been in France when the people confronted their oppressors. It is significant that the only part of The Prelude tobe published in Wordsworth's lifetime was the famous pro-revolutionary extract from Book

X. claimed James. K Chandler [29].

> *'O pleasant exercise of hope and joy!*
> *For mighty were the auxiliaries which then*
> *stood Upon our side, us who were strong in*
> *love!*
> *Bliss was it in that dawn to be alive,*
> *But to be young was very Heaven! O*
> *times, In which the meagre, stale,*
> *forbidding ways Of custom, law, and*
> *statute, took at once The attraction of a*
> *country in romance!*
> *When Reason seemed the most to assert her rights*
> *When most intent on making of herself*
> *A prime enchantress—to assist the work,*
> *Which then was going forward in her*
> *name!'* [30].

---

[29] See Chandler, James K *Wordsworth's Second Nature: A Study in the Poetry and Politics* (Chicago, University of Chicago Press, 1984) p 46-7.
[30] Wordsworth, William *The Major Works* (Oxford, Oxford University Press, 2000) p.548

Nigel Pearce

It will be argued that a radical British working-class tendency was impacted upon by the political and cultural effects of the French revolution. Although there was a Jacobean moment in Britain it took a far more advanced form in Ireland with an organized insurrection by the United Irishmen in 1798 which was brutally and bloodily suppressed on the orders of Lord Castlereagh. He would also be responsible for the Peterloo Massacre outside of Manchester in 1819. Shelley felt driven to write The Mask of Anarchy *after the bloodletting in Manchester:*

> *As I lay asleep in Italy*
> *There came a voice from over the Sea,*
> *And with great power it forth led me*
> *To walk in the visions of Poesy.*
>
> *I met Murder on the way-*
> *He had a mask like Castlereagh-*
> *Very smooth he looked, yet grim;*
> *Seven blood-hounds followed him:*
>
> *All were fat; and well they*
> *might Be in admirable plight,*
> *For one by one, and two by two,*
> *He tossed the human hearts to chew*
> *Which from his wide cloak he drew* [31]

Lord Byron's assaults on Castlereagh were if anything, more belligerent and bellicose than Shelley's denunciation of the massacre at Peterloo, an early suffrage gathering. Byron used both cutting satire and something boarding on 'hatred' of colonial oppression as he scribed these lines about the Irish Uprising of 1798 and its consequences in The 'Dedication to Don Juan':

> *The intellectual eunuch Castlereagh...*
> *Cold-blooded, smooth-faced, placid miscreant*
> *Dabbling its sleek young hands in Erin's gore.* [32][32]

I shall illustrate in Chapter Three the importance of the colonial rule of Britain in Ireland to Chartism and its poetry. Hence, we can comprehend a pro-revolutionary propensity amongst both first and second-generation Romantic poets who had benefited from the emergent industrial complex, capitalism, in one way or another and then turned their pens against capitalism's excesses. Nevertheless, as Karl Marx speculated about Shelley, he was the only one of them who was a 'thourghgoing revolutionary and would always have belonged to the Socialist vanguard.' [33]

---

[31] Shelley, Percy Bysshe, *The Major Works* (Oxford, Oxford University Press, 2003) p.400.
[32] Byron, Lord *The Major Works* (Oxford, Oxford University Press, 2008) p.375-376.
[33] Marx, Karl & Engels Frederick *Literature and Art: Selections from Their Writings* (New York, International Publishers, 1947) p. 132.

The case of William Wordsworth, as I argued, was intriguing. He was possibly the most read of the major Romantic poets by the bourgeoisie. As he lived throughout the period it was possible to gauge his writing against a protracted and turbulent period of working-class struggle. The French Revolution was in nature a bourgeois revolution. However, in England change was also in the air and it would spawn the London Corresponding Society, which at its height had 3,000 paid-members.[34] *The Pitt government feared revolution and put the leadership on trial for High Treason for which they were acquitted. However, a defence fund was created and a 'Citizen Wordsworth' contributed 1s - 0d.*[35] *In A Letter to the Bishop of Llandaff (1793) Wordsworth echoed Thomas Paine: 'Political convulsions have been said particularly to call forth concealed abilities...'*[36] *See Thomas Paine, Rights of Man, II. 420:*

> *It appears to general observation, that revolutions create genius and talents; but those events do no more than bring them forward. There is existing in man, a mass of sense lying in a dormant state.*[37]

As late as 1821 Wordsworth argued when asked by James Losh about his changed political opinions, the middle-aged poet answered:

> *If I were addressing those who have dealt so liberally with the words Renegade Apostate, etc., I should retort the charge upon them, and say, you have been deluded by Places and Persons, while I have stuck to Principles — I abandoned France, and her Rulers, when they abandoned the struggle for Liberty, gave themselves up to Tyranny, and endeavoured to enslave the world.*[38]

After the planting of what E.P. Thompson called 'The Liberty Tree'[39]. *A metaphor for an incipient wave of proletarian class struggle in Britain, followed by the biting chill of reaction and then the rise of a new wave of hope and struggle in the guise of Chartism. Thomas Carlyle in his essay Chartism (1839) raised the "Condition of England Question" I.e. mass poverty and alienation amongst the working class which he believed was caused by lassie- faire capitalism, Mammonism in the aristocracy and scientific materialism. He too feared the English proletariat would create a revolution.*

However, another theoretical tendency was spreading its tentacles into its natural subject, it's world-historic subject, the proletariat. Engels was the first of the two

---

[34] Hunt, Jocelyn B. *Understanding the London Corresponding Society a Balancing Act between Adversaries Thomas Paine and Edmund Burke.* Thesis. University of Waterloo, 2013. pp. 1-13.

[35] Pamphlet entitled *London Corresponding Society,* Nov 19th, 1794 (1795) p.5

[36] *Wordsworth, William. Wordsworth's Political Writings (Kindle Locations 1097-1099). Humanities-eBooks. Kindle Edition.*

[37] Wordsworth, William. *Wordsworth's Political Writings* (Kindle Locations 8149-8150). Humanities-eBooks. Kindle Edition

[38] Wordsworth, W. *The letters of William and Dorothy Wordsworth: The later years, 1821-1853* (2nd ed.) (Vols. 1-4). (Oxford, Oxford University Press, 1978-1988), I: 97.

[39] Thompson, E.P. *The Making of the English Working Class* (London, Penguin, 1991) p.111.

founders of scientific socialism as opposed to utopian socialism to comment[40] Engels would write: 'These six points harmless as they seem, are sufficient to overthrow the whole English Constitution, Queen and Lords included.'[41] This was because he understood them as transitional demands, i.e. neither stressing mere reformist or exaggerating any revolutionary potential in the context of that place and time and, therefore, able to mobilize workers to seek the contestation of state power. He understood this to be their historically necessary task. The Chartists' Six Demands which were set out in the Crown and Anchor public house on 28th February 1837 by William Lovett on behalf of The London Workingman's Association:

- A vote for every man twenty-one years of age, of sound mind, and not under going *punishment for a crime.*
- The secret ballot to protect the elector in the exercise of his vote.

- No property qualification for Members of Parliament in order to allow the constituencies to return the man of their choice.
- Payment of Members, enabling tradesmen, working men, or other persons of modest means to leave or interrupt their livelihood to attend to the interests of the nation.

- Equal constituencies, securing the same amount of representation for the same number of electors, instead of allowing less populous constituencies to have as much or more weight than larger ones.
- Annual Parliamentary elections, thus presenting the most effectual check to bribery and intimidation, since no purse could buy a constituency under a system of universal manhood suffrage in each twelve-month period.

Leon Trotsky, who maintained the English Revolution and the Chartists laid bare the myth of English gradualism suggested that class struggle is central to the creation of art:

> *Generally speaking, art is an expression of man's need for a harmonious and complete life, that is to say, his need for those major benefits of which a society of classes has deprived him. That is why a protest against reality, either conscious or unconscious, active or passive, optimistic or pessimistic, always forms part of a really creative piece of work. Every new tendency in art has begun with rebellion.[42]*

We would see that a new dialectic of the class would create not only something quantitatively new but a dialectical leap to a qualitatively different situation with the masses. It was a 'leap 'but also had a linear nature. An inheritance from previous working-class struggles in the form of an organized working class press for which there was a material base. Ulrich Schwab commented there was 'a demand for

---

[40] See Engels, Fredrick *Socialism: Utopian or Scientific* (*London*, Bookmarks, 1993)
[41] Marx, Karl & Engels, Frederick *Collected Works in 50 volumes*, vol 4, p.518 (New York, International Publishers, 2004).
[42] https://www.marxist.com/art-politics-our-epoch-tro sky080107

serious reading material amongst the workers.' [43] *The response of the British state apparatus in 1815 was to try and suppress the workers' press with stamp duty. It became known as 'a Tax on knowledge' and several radical papers went underground. Notably, Black Dwarf launched by Thomas Wooler in 1817 which frequently quoted William Shakespeare . Also, of note was ThePoorman's Guardian 1831-1835 was founded by Henry Hetherington as a successor to his earlier (1830–31) penny daily Penny Papers for the People, as an outright challenge to authority. Published at the low price of a penny per weekly copy it bore the politically provocative heading: 'Published contrary to 'law' to try the power of 'might' against 'right'' Nevertheless, the working-class press was variable and certainly in periods of low class struggle was sentimental and sensationalist. Looking at the growth of a class-based literature in the nineteenth century generally, Martha Vicinus argued its "variety grew out of many long-developing political and social movements.'* [44]

Why did Chartism become a movement sustained by poetry? I address many of the practical questions in Chapter Two. One answer is that unlike the discourse of the 'big six' of Romanticism it was a cross-generic phenomenon. It was not disciplined by a learning based in Latin and Greek, although as Thomas Hardy later understood in Jude the Obscure, many workers aspired to a classical education. However, Jude the Obscure describes a period of low class struggle and hence the atomized worker, it is great literature though. Nevertheless, if we briefly examine two other revolutionary moments and recall Thomas Paine and Leon Trotsky as above on revolution and art from The Rights of Man (1791) and Art and Politics in Our Epoch (1938) respectively. The analytical apparatus for an argument becomes apparent, the masses and their poets rebelled. There have always been poets as Caudwell argued they had existed as priests and shamans.
However, independently of Caudwell we can understand an insight from Walter Benjamin.
The Work of Art in the Age of Mechanical Reproduction (2008 [1936]). Here he illustrates the nature of modernization on the artistic process:

> *The work of art when it can be reproduced by*
> *Technological means... the technological means*
> *frees the work of art, for the first time in history,*
> *from its existence as a parasite upon ritual.* [45]

He concluded one should argue that: 'Communism's reply is to politicize art' (2008 [1936])

---

[43] Schwab, Ulrich *The poetry of the Chartist Movement: A Literary and Historical Study*(Dordrecht: Kluwer Academic Publishers, 1987) p. 27.

[44] Vicinus, Martha, *The Industrial Muse: A Study of Nineteenth Century Working-Class Literature* (London, Croom Helm, 1974), p.94.

[45] Benjamin, Walter *The Work of Art in the Age of Mechanical Reproduction* (London, Penguin Great Ideas, 2008 [1936]) pp. 11-12.

p. 38. We see the rise of mass culture. Another reason the Chartists wrote poetry was an established tradition of street ballads. In the words of Malcolm Chase:

> *Poetry mattered to the Chartists, especially after November 1839 [the defeat of the Newport uprising]. Verse, rather than the speaker's platform or journalism, was the safest public space wherein to proclaim revolutionary sentiment. To write and read (especially aloud) or sing verse was also to confront polite culture. It located Chartism within an intellectual and political tradition that extended back to the English Revolution; Milton and Marvel were amongst the most popular models for Chartist poetry.* [46]

But what of my barometer of the period in England, William Wordsworth, and the concept of 'Jacobinism-in-recoil'. I hope that I have intimated that might not have been a totally satisfactory reading. I looked to John Williams Wordsworth: Romantic Poetry and Revolution (1989) who argued William Wordsworth was after all thinking consistently and this could be explained by employing the Gramscian category 'of a traditional intellectual'. As Antonio Gramsci maintained of the 'traditional intellectual':

> *'He is seeking intellectual categories which were pre-existing, and which, moreover, appeared as representatives of an historical continuity uninterrupted even by the most complicated and radical changes, of social and political forms.* [47]

This may seem a little rigid and harsh, but it reflects William Wordsworth's class orientation. He might well have sympathized, yet more, he did feel an empathy with the rural poor and toyed with revolution, but he was never going to mount the barricades. Rather Antonio Gramsci's concept of the 'organic intellectual' is of explanatory value when examining Chartist poets. He had argued:

> *That all men are intellectuals, in that all have intellectual and rational faculties, but not all men have the social function of intellectuals* [48]

So, for Gramsci working class or 'organic intellectuals' contest the ruling-class hegemony in 'a war of manoeuvre' with 'traditional intellectuals' until the time is ripe for 'social revolution'. We can understand Chartist poets as examples of 'organic

---

[46] Chase. Malcolm *Chartism: A New History* (Manchester, Manchester University Press, 2007) p.118.

[47] Gramsci, Antonio 'The Formation of Intellectuals' in *The Modern Prince and Other Writings (New York, International Publishers, 1978), p, 119.*

[48] Gramsci, Antonio Selections *from the Prison Notebooks.* (London, Lawrence and Wishart, 1982) p.8.

intellectuals' challenging the bourgeois dominance with their material, the poetry. As here in the concluding lines of Ernest Jones' poem:

The Cornfield and the Factory.

*The very sun shines pale on a dark earth,
Where quivering engines groan their horrid
mirth, And black smoke-offerings, crimes and
curses, swell From furnace-altars of incarnate
hell!
The demon laughs, and still his arm he
waves, That thins the villages but fills the
graves.
Through bleak, deserted fields he loves to roam,
Where shines the furnace on hell's harvest-
home. 'Tis this has stilled the laughter of the
child,
And made man's mirth less holy, but more wild!
Bade Heav'n's pure light from woman's eye
depart, And trodden love from out her gentle
heart.
'Tis this, that wards the sunshine from the sod...* [49]

'The Factory Town' which was in ballad form while 'The Cornfield and the Town' was an experimental poem written later and published in a book rather than a worker's newspaper. Ernest Jones was still a convinced socialist but his parlance and the troupes he employshad altered. The reader still comprehended a dichotomy between town and country. However, a 'demon laughs' which is a metaphor not only for industrial pollution but also his demonic effluence generally. He is spewing fire, brimstone, smoke and evil. Thus, the speaker can terrify and depopulate: 'thin the villages' and 'fill the graves'. Jones uses alliteration quite convincingly 'hell's harvest home'. The addressee feels flung into the Inferno. Then the poem becomes a morality tale as man is 'made more wild' and 'Heav'n's pure light from women's eyes depart.' A very Victorian gender stereotyping. Even 'the very smile of God' as one would have expected in Hell does not penetrate. It is certainly not Dante. However, Jones is endeavouring not to use the language of current social strife here. Rather for him that period was in limbo as he had broken with Marx and Engels over the question of revolutionaries agitating in the new trade union movement. So, it is consistent that he would harness the registers of Evangelical Christianity to further his ends. Although unlike Thomas Cooper he had not eschewed his revolutionary beliefs.
Indeed, he is still contesting hegemony but not with the language concomitant with a heightened period of class struggle.

---

[49] Jones, Ernest *The Battle-Day and Other Poems* (London, Routledge & Co, 1855). p. 93-94.

Nigel Pearce

Chapter Two.

Contrasting Chartist publications and perspectives on poetry.

An orthodoxy had been created in the first anthologies of Chartist literature. e.g. (Yuri Kovalev, 1956)[50]. It was originally used for teaching in the USSR. Then published in the West by Central Books with his analysis, in Russian, translated at Manchester University two years later. It was published later that year in the U.S.A, Victorian Studies Vol. 2, No. 2 (December 1958). His argument was that Chartist poetry had almost 'mechanistically' arisen out of the period which the Victorians came to call Romanticism and then developed its own character. However, he was weak in many areas e.g. mechanistic materialism rather than dialectical materialism, a lack of weight given to John Ruskin's influence on William Morris to mention two errors. His analysis has endured, in one manifestation or another, until recently. As with all theoretical models it required readjustment and revisiting of the primary texts in the hope of devising new solutions and the possibility of opening up new areas of research. Hence a more complex narrative has now emerged. Kovalev's pioneering anthology and the question of the centrality of Romanticism to the Chartist poetic is a debate which has been reanimated in recent years. There is doubtlessly an echo of Romanticism in Chartist poetics. The question is whether they were able to make a dialectical leap into something innovatory. An autonomous literature is another question.

An important area in the evaluation of labouring-class poetics is its limitations, strengths and futures.

For the Chartists, literature and especially poetry were of huge significance. As Malcolm Chase made clear 'Chartist poets aspired to a greater sophistication than the street balladeers of the time, successfully so.'[51] The Chartist Circular (1839- 1842) and The Labourer (1847-1848) espoused contradictory ideas about working- class poetry argued (Sanders, 2013). I will examine that relationship but also by extension Feargus O'Connor's mighty The Northern Star (1837-1852) which was the literary spine of the Chartist movement. This is revealing because Feargus O'Connor was the proprietor of The Northern Star and co-owner and editor of The Labourer with Ernest Jones in 1847-8. Hence, we can comprehend how the perspectives on poetry changed over a longer period within Chartism and in more detail. Although neither Thomas Cooper nor Ernest Jones wrote for The Chartist Circular. Mainly lesser known and often anonymous writers did, and this will facilitate a deeper understanding of the relationship between Romanticism which was the dominant genre within The Chartist Circular and the earlier Chartist movement. We will perceive a shift in the aftermath of the failure of the 1842 General Strike away from a working-class adherence to Romanticism towards a harsher, poetic realism. That is, the poet was no longer seen

---

[50] Kovalev, Y. *An anthology of Chartist Literature* (Moscow, Foreign Languages Publishing House,1956).
[51] Chase, Malcolm (2007) p.119

as the genius through which poetry came into being (Wordsworth, Introduction to Lyrical Ballads 1802) albeit in the language of the common people or the poets 'as the unacknowledged legislators of the world.' (Shelley, In Defence of Poetry, 1832). The poet became the activist whom through which the oppressed will achieve a communitarian and equitable social formation. Thus, the first wave of Chartist writers would become the mouthpieces of what Thomas Cooper called 'Knowledge, the great Enfranchiser' (Randell,1999, p.184). This suggested that the future of labouring-class poetry could be, not merely a vehicle for winning the vote, but more ambitious. One aspiration suggested by Thomas Cooper was 'a language of our own.' Meaning a distinct and articulate discourse dialectically opposed to the varied and competing narrative of poets like Elizabeth Barrett Browning, Robert Browning, Alfred Tennyson, Mathew Arnold and, at the time, marginalized writers like Christina Rossetti and later the Jesuit priest, Gerald Manley Hopkins. However, for working-class poets like the young Thomas Cooper and increasingly so with Ernest Jones didactic poetry to suit an epoch and the Chartist struggle would become the norm. Interestingly both Marx and Engels argued against a simplistic tendentious poetry and admired Shakespeare, Schiller, Byron, Shelley and Heinrich Heine who was a friend.

The Northern Star was by far the most successful of the Chartist newspapers or journals achieving a circulation of 50,000 at its peak during the Birmingham Riots in July 1839.[52] At times between 1838-52 the poetry editors were sometimes so inundated with poetry that:

> *we have received so much poetry as a donkey could draw and [are] gutted with almost as a jackass had what claims to be poetry waiting for them.[53]*

It claimed a verbal range of seven per copy being read aloud by literate workers to their illiterate comrades. This exhibited a high level of solidarity. The Northern Star of Leeds, a weekly, as I mentioned became the backbone of Chartism was founded by Feargus O'Connor who in 1837 had named it after the Ulster paper of the insurrectionary nationalist group the United Irishmen. They had risen nationally under the leadership of a Protestant Wolfe Tone and been suppressed by the British in 1798. O'Connor was imprisoned for a 'seditious libel' in 1839 written in The Northern Star and upon his release from York Castle Prison in 1841 The Lion of Freedom was first sung, composed by Thomas Cooper. Cooper was a fascinating man. He would be imprisoned in 1842 during the General Strike for inciting a riot. The Lion of Freedom became a very popular poetic song and was often roared wherever Feargus O'Connor appeared. Although later in his life Thomas Cooper would deny it was composed by him or as Edward Royle claimed.[54]

---

[52] Epstein, James *The Lion of Freedom* (London, Breviary Stuff Publications 2015) p.59.

[53] *Northern Star*, 1st January 1842.

[54] Royle, Edward *Chartism* (London, Longman, (1996) p.108.

Nigel Pearce

"The Lion of Freedom,"

*'Lion of Freedom is come from his
den; We'll rally around him, again
and again:
We'll crown him with laurel, our champion to be:
O'Connor the patriot: for sweet Liberty!*

*The pride of the people—He's noble and
brave— A terror to tyrants—a friend to the
slave:
The bright star of Freedom—the noblest of
men: We'll rally around him, again and
again.*

*Who strove for the patriots—was up night and
day— To save them from falling to tyrants a
prey?
'Twas fearless O'Connor was diligent then:
We'll rally around him, again and again.*

*Though proud daring tyrants his body
confined, They never could conquer his
generous mind: We'll hail our caged lion, now
freed from his den: We'll rally around him,
again and again.
-Thomas Cooper.* [55]

*Thomas Cooper wrote of O'Connor in his autobiography: 'The popularity of this song
may serve to show how firmly O'Connor was fixed in the regard of a portion of the
manufacturing operatives, as the incorruptible advocate of freedom. Therefore, they
immediately suspected the honesty of any local leader who did not rank himself under
the banner of Feargus, the leader-in-chief. I note the that this poetic song was used in
'performance' for rousing the spirits of the masses and Thomas Cooper described it as
a 'chant'. It is in ballad form, four quatrains rhyming aabb with a pronounced
anaphora "We'll rally" which one can imagine whipped-up emotion in large
audiences. Thomas Cooper could read out loud from the age of three:*
  *Thomas Cooper had his first encounter with Byron's poetry: in
  my thirteenth year, by some accident there fell into my hands one*

---

[55] Cooper, Thomas The Northern Star (1841).

of the cantos of Childe Harold's Pilgrimage and the drama of Manfred. I had them in my hands for only a few hours, and I knew nothing of their noble author's life or reputation, but they seemed to create a new sense within me. I wanted more poetry to read from that time but could get hold of none that thrilled through my nature like Byron's. A couple of years later as an apprentice shoemaker, Cooper was introduced to the poetry of Burns by his master. As with Somerville, the effect was exhilarating – 'The pathos of Burns took possession of my whole nature almost as completely as the fire and force of Byron. [56]

I shall undertake an analysis of 'The Poetry Column' of The Northern Star 1838–1852 with the statistics found by Sanders (2009, p71). By way of an interpretation, I note Thomas Julian Harney was appointed editor in 1843 and after his ideological disagreement with Feargus O'Connor over the influence of Marx and Engels the paper moved to London in 1844. The Northern Star went into relative decline after the revolutions of 1848 as shown in the number of poems published. We can also ascertain that after the failure of the General Strike in 1842 within two years the division between 'non-Chartist produced poems' and poems written by Chartists takes approximately half each. Whereas previously the Chartist poetry was in the ascendency. This I suggest reflected the division of labour between manual and mental labour which the young Marx in 1844 had seen at the heart of human alienation that is inherent in capitalism:

Estranged labour not only (1) estranges nature from man and (2) man from himself, from his own function, from his vital activity; because of this it also estranges man from his own species. It turns his species-life into a means for his individual life. Firstly, it estranges species-life and individual life, and secondly, it turns the latter in its abstract form, into the purpose for the former, also in its abstract form and estranged form. [57]

This was a breakthrough, I would argue, for the way we comprehend our species-being or essence. What Marx had done was lift the veil on why the worker feels alienated from their labour or species-being under the circumstances of early capitalism, why they felt estranged from nature and each other. William Morris after recognizing his indebtedness to John Ruskin would later advocate Socialism as the only solution to this malady:

Yet it may be remembered that civilisation has reduced the working man to such a skinny and pitiable existence...It is the province of art to set the true ideal of a full and reasonable life before him, a life in which the

---

[56] Cooper, Thomas *The Life of Thomas Cooper* (London, Hodder & Stoughton, 1873,) p.176
[57] Marx, Karl *Early Writings* (London, Pelican Marx Library,1977) p.328.

perception and creation of beauty, the enjoyment of real pleasure that is, shall be felt as necessary to man as his daily bread.[58]

Here, I suggest, William Morris is delineating a complex aesthetic, one that synthesises the dialectical opposites of labour and literature. This was a seminal moment for modern aesthetics as it created an organic human unity and the possibility of living without alienation. With the revolutionary wave of 1848 and the interest was again, it seemed, centred on London after rioting, the mass meeting on Kennington Green of 200,000 and the Third Petition. This was foiled by O'Connor's huge error in judgement in not marching on parliament. It created an audience for the Left though. I will examine the 'Left Turn' and its ramifications for poetry in Chapter Three

Mike Sanders (2013) argued the earlier Chartist publication The Chartist Circular had been under the influence of Romanticism. The Chartist Circular had maintained a position in favour of bourgeois democracy or suffrage as understood in the original Six Point Charter and was also in favour of the creation of a 'National Poetry.' A front page from The Chartist Circular: edited by William Thompson was openly class-collaborationist. It was not a newspaper in the sense The Northern Star and The Labourer were 'but an educational journal…throughout the paper's life it had a quote from the Marquis de Lafayette as its masthead: For a Nation to Love Liberty, it is sufficient that she knows it: and to be free, it is sufficient that she wills it.'

W. Hamish Frasier points out:

> *From the start, there was an appeal to the middle classes, whom Whig governments 'had treated with contempt', and, an appeal to 'the industrial classes' who had carried the Reform Act…Only the union of our middle-class and working classes could affect to regenerate the country…*[61]

The Chartist Circular which was published in Glasgow at its peak sold 20,000 copies and had two poetry columns. The first *The Politics of Poetry* existed between 11th January 1839 -March 13th, 1840. This was followed by Literary Sketches from 11th June 1840- April 9th, 1842. During the whole period, it published around 150 poems by at least 67 poets while The Northern Star published around 350 poems by at least 120 poets. So, in literary terms, it was a significant publication. As Mike Sanders maintained 'it can be argued that poetry played an even more significant role in The Chartist Circular than it did in The Northern Star. In its first comment on the nature of poetry The Chartist Circular noted:

> *The gentleman critics complain that the union of poetry with politics is always hurtful to the politics, and fatal to the poetry. But these great connoisseurs must be wrong, if Homer, Dante, Shakespeare, Milton, Cowper, and Burns were poets.*

---

[58] Morris, William *Useful Work v, Useless Toil* (London, Penguin Books, Great Ideas, 2008) p.93-4.

('The Politics of Poets, No. 1', 1840, p. 170.[59]

Mike Sanders echoed Anne Janowitz's earlier scholarship linking Romanticism and Chartism which is central to my work. Mike Sanders observed this theme in The Chartist Circular: 'Shelley, Byron, Wordsworth, Coleridge and the young Southey are all discussed and praised for their Republican and/or democratic tendencies.' [60]*Wecan also note that the early stanzas of Book 2 Thomas Cooper's The Purgatory of Suicides positions his poetry in a national dialogue including Shakespeare, Milton, Sydney, Byron, a 'National Bard'. I would note a dialectic here between the objective class position of the poets idealized and that of the Chartist poets who elevated them. This can be perceived as a form of estrangement in the same way as when humanity project their 'species- being' onto an external object in much the same way Ludwig Feuerbach had argued the 'alienated' human beings projected their essence onto a God in the heavens and thus lost an element of their humanity.* [61]

Is it possible to create an independent working-class literature within the confines of capitalism? I argue in a similar vein to Leon Trotsky in Class and Art (1924) that the possibility of a pre-revolutionary proletarian class literature is small until Socialism is created. I think the forces both objective and subjective are so immense and, indeed, corrosive to the proletarian poet under capitalism. She or he is exploited, alienated and exhausted by labour. Indeed, the question of whether the Chartist workers' movement of 1836-52 was class-conscious to the extent of having metamorphosed from being what Marx described as a 'class-in-itself' into the heightened revolutionary state of being a 'class-for- itself' is one that is unresolved even amongst Marxian commentators e.g. Gareth Steadman-Jones *Language of Class: Studies in English working-class history [Rethinking Chartism, 1983], pp 90-177* for a thoughtful but totally Revisionist reading and Dorothy Thompson. *The Chartists* (London, Breviary Stuff Publications, 2013) for a slightly less Revisionist reading but one that mistakenly understands the Marxist theory of history as teleological rather than dialectical.

However, the literary pages of The Labourer, under the control of Ernest Jones, were championing the world-view of the proletariat which is, I argue, internationalist. It was, therefore, suggested that only from a future communal society could a working class or mass poetic be drawn in the pages of The Labourer. Two contributions by Ernest Jones from that publication illustrate that there was also meaningful and profound literary criticism being written and read in the Chartist movement:

> *There are class poets, the same as we have class-legislators. They seize some topic interesting only to the privileged few, or, more frequently, dwell on morbid, abstract theories, that never can claim, nor even deserve general attention.*

---

[59] *Class and the Canon: Constructing Labouring-Class Poetry and Poetics, 1780-1900* (p. 157). Palgrave
[60] Frasier. Hamish (2005) p.92
[61] See Feuerbach, Ludwig The *Essence of Christianity,* trans George Elliot.

- Ernest Jones, 1847a, p. 284. [62]

And also:

> *[Chartist] poetry is, indeed the freshest and most stirring of the age; as in England, thus in France, America, Ireland, and Germany, the poetic spirit has struck the chords of liberty, and the fresh vigour of its production's contrasts proudly with the emasculated verses of a fashionable school. Yet, for many, we have expected more. What is Robert Browning doing? He, who could fire the soul of a Luria, and develop the characters of a Victor and a Charles, – he, who could depict nature's nobility in a Colombe, – has he nothing to say for popular rights? Let him eschew his kings and queens, – let him quit the pageantry of courts – and ascend into the cottage of the poor. Can Tennyson do no more than troll a courtly lay? His oak could tell other tales besides a love story.*
>
> - *Ernest Jones, 1847b, pp. 95–6.* [63]

We understand a clear aesthetic judgement made by a man who had been a lawyer and had originated from an aristocratic background. I postulate that he would have probably had a knowledge of Kantian aesthetics and ideas of literary taste. He would certainly have been aware of John Keats Ode to a Grecian Urn from his pre-Chartist period:

> *When old age shall this generation waste*
> *Thou shalt remain, in midst of other woe*
> *Than ours, a friend to man, to whom thou*
> * sayst, "Beauty is truth, truth beauty," – that is*
> * all*
> *Ye know on earth, and all ye need to know. (lines 46–50)* [67]

What we are really looking at here is the beginning of the formation of Nations and simultaneously canonizing of English poetry and prose. As Terry Eagleton argued:

> *It is no accident that the period we are discussing [the second half of the eighteenth century, leading into the Romantic period] sees the rise of modern 'aesthetics'. ... It is mainly from this era, in the work of Kant, Hegel, Schiller, Coleridge and others, that we inherit our contemporary ideas of ... 'aesthetic experience', of 'aesthetic harmony' and the unique nature of the artefact...*

---

[62] Jones, Ernest (1847a) 'Review: T. Powell', *The Labourer*, 1:6, 284.
[63] Ernest Jones The Labourer

Now, this concrete, historically variable practices were being subsumed into some special, mysterious faculty known as the 'aesthetic'.... Art was extricated from the material practices, social relations and ideological meanings in which it is always caught up and raised to the status of a solitary fetish.[64]

The endurance of beauty is a powerful metaphor in Keats' 1819 'Ode to a Grecian Urn' and would have impacted on the pre-Chartist reading of Ernest Jones. But when the knock is hard on the door of History there is a sharpening of class divisions and class-consciousness. By 1843 Engels and then Marx was intensely involved in the Chartist movement and their thinking about literature would have been an influence on Ernest Jones. Indeed, Marx in his analysis of the European revolutions of 1848 concluded: 'The social revolution cannot take its poetry from the past, only the future.' Nevertheless, the process of incipient 'canon-building' with the rise of the bourgeois nation-state and its consolidation were both factors, I suggest, in the marginalisation of labouring-class poetry. Indeed, in making it a 'hidden history.'

In Britain, the poetry of Chartism was by the dawn of the European revolutions taking a harsher tone as here in Ernest Jones poem about those who betray their class. Here we perceive an upper class or professional poet who is aligned with the Chartists using onomatopoeia to convey the sense of the proletariat 'policing' their own communities. This is a phenomenon which occurred in working-class communities during periods of high 'class consciousness' or when power was contested between the proletariat and bourgeoisie e.g., 'dual power' in Russia between February and October 1917 or Catalonia during the Spanish Civil War in 1937 when there was a revolution within a civil war. Equally, at a lower level during the Miners' Strike of 1984-85 in British pit villages. Here in The Labourer, Vol 2, 1848 and I note that this poem is almost excluded from two recent 'polite' studies of Ernest Jones. Only a cursory remark is made by Miles Taylor[65]. It is completely ignored by Simon Rennie.[66]

THE SONG OF THE GAGGERS.

Gag—gag—gag!
Is the cry of the traitor
band,
While they try, with a printed
rag, To ride like a midnight hag
On the breast of a sleeping land.

---

[64] Eagleton, Terry *Literary Theory: An Introduction* (Oxford, Blackwell, 1996) pp 18-19.

[65] Taylor, Miles Ernest Jones, Chartism and the Romance of Politics 1819-1869 (Oxford, Oxford University Press, 2003) p.112.

[66] Rennie, Simon The Poetry of Ernest Jones: Myth, Song and the 'Mighty Mind' (Routledge, London, 2016).

Come—knave and villain, informer and
spy, To the government mint, where you
coin a lie! Gold—gold—gold!
Is the pay for the ready slave,
Whose word at a breath can destroy the
bold, In the halls where justice is bought
and sold, And the withering glance falls
keen and cold On the heart of the true and
brave.

Gag—gag—gag!
Is the cry of the traitor band
While they try, with a printed
rag, To ride like a midnight
hag
On the breast of a sleeping land.

We'll stay the stream in its fullest force,
We'll stop the world in its onward
course— Gag—gag—gag!
The voice of six thousand years
Shall begin at our bidding to fail and flag
Not a lip shall breathe, not a tongue shall
wag And history's page be an idle brag,
Compared to Russell's fears.

Gag—gag—gag! Is the cry of the traitor
band, While they seek with a printed rag,
To ride like a midnight hag,
On the breast of a sleeping land.

In vain shall the blood of an Emmett have
flowed, In vain shall the breast of a miser have
glowed!
Gag—Gag—Gag!
The thought in the teeming brain!
The pulse in the heart of the world shall
lag, And nations the burden of misery drag,
And Lilliput trample on
Brobdingnag. As long as a Russell
shall reign.

- Ernest Jones.

The refrain repeated is four times with trimeter of choking 'heavy' or strong poetic 'feet' as the speaker hands out class justice to the class traitor. This rather predictably changes from Gag-gag-gag to Gold-gold-gold/Is the pay for the ready slave. However, the alliterative 'g' sounds do sustain an atmosphere of threat. Of note, because Feargus O'Connor was the proprietor and co-editor of The Labourer, is Ernest Jones couplet where he links class treachery to internationalism with the Jonathon Swift allusion. Gulliver's Travels was written in Ireland. This is important because Ernest Jones was moving rapidly Leftwards and adopting an internationalist proletarian worldview. Therefore, he was involved with an organization called the Fraternal Democrats who were founded at a meeting held in London on September 22th, 1845. The society embraced representatives of Left Chartists and emigres with which Marx and Engels were closely involved and it was the precursor to the First International eventually created with the assistance of Marx and Engels in 1864. We understand an echo of both Byron's and Shelley's support for the anti-imperialist struggles and those of the poor. Also contrast the literary allusions in Ernest Jones poem to Swift's Gulliver's Travels, complex satire, in comparison with Thomas Coopers' more popular The Lion of Freedom. The poem had earned Cooper the title 'the Chartist Laurette' together with his The Purgatory of Suicides: A Prison-Rhyme (1845). It was a political epic of 922 Spenserian stanzas. By 1846, he had broken with O'Connor and became a 'moral force' Chartist. The latter was very different from his earlier poetry and illustrates an attempted shift in Thomas Cooper from working-class autodidact to rise to the level of a middle-class professional poet. He was the model for the central character in Charles Kingsley's Industrial Novel Alton Locke (1850).

Although the tensions between Ernest Jones and Feargus O'Connor were not fraught at that time argued Glenn Aire who commented: 'The Labourer more so than even The Northern Star was a palpably O'Connoirite journal.'[67] *However, there is documentary evidence that suggests the two men were not so aligned ideologically. I can illustrate that Ernest Jones gravitated towards Chartism in late 1845. 'In the winter of 1845, having accidentally seen a copy of the Northern Star, and finding the political principles advocated harmonized with my own, I sought the executive and joined the Chartist movement.'*[68] *This made it inevitable he would meet George Harney who Paul Foot showed was a worker and an autodidact. His radical agitation could be traced all the way back to the 'Stamp Wars', the struggle for a worker's press.*[69] *George Harney recorded his first meeting with Engels in 1843. 'It was in 1843 that he came over from Bradford from Leeds and enquired for me at The Northern Star office...He told me he was a constant reader of The Northern Star and took a keen interest in the Chartist movement. Thus, began our friendship over fifty years ago.'*[70] *John Saville in his definitive Marxist study of Ernest Jones is absolutely clear, Marx*

---

[67] Jones, *The Labourer*,1846

[68] Airey, Glenn Feargus O'Connor, Ernest Jones and The Labourer in [ed] Allen, Joan and Ashton. An Owen *Papers for The People A Study of the Chartist Press* (London, The Merlin Press, 2005) p.120

[69] Saville, John Ernest *Jones Chartist* (London, Lawrence & Wishart, 1952) p.17.

[70] Foot, Paul, *The Vote* (London, Bookmarks, 2012). pp. 89-90.

and Jones met in November 1847.[71] *Thus, it is difficult to deny the persuasiveness of V. I. Lenin 's position when he argued the Chartist movement was at least from 1843 onwards 'the first genuinely mass revolutionary movement' and 'the word but one before Marxism'. That is not to argue there were no other factions; variants on 'moral force' Chartism. Decent people who believed the working class needed only education and the vote alone to acquire State power. However, the extremely wealthy and their cohorts in the state apparatus will not give up power to another class unless compelled too.*

It is clear following the most recent scholarship i.e., Sanders, Janowitz and Margaret

A. Loose that the role of poetry in the Chartist movement was ideological so people were not being introspective. There would have been time for that if they had created a new Commonwealth or, equally, The New Jerusalem, Socialism but they failed. This failure and its consequences for a British working-class poetic will be addressed in the next chapter. I have illustrated that poetry and literary criticism were prevalent in the Chartist press. I had shown a drift to the Marxist 'Left' from an explicitly class collaborationist journal through to one that published the first English edition of Marx & Engels Communist Manifesto. We saw how dialectical conflict is at the heart of History and how writing reflected these conflicts. I have made a case for the simultaneous rise of the modern bourgeoisie in Britain and the incipient process of creating a literary Canon. This was captured in 1872 by Mathew Arnold: "Culture, the ac quainting ourselves with the best that has been known and said in the and thus with the history of the human spirits.'[77] *This has inevitably left 'hidden histories' for scholars to explore.*

---

[71] *Reminiscences of Marx and Engels* (Moscow, Foreign Languages Publishing House, 1963). p.192.

Chapter Three.

1848, the 'Left Turn' and the poetry of class struggle.

This chapter will examine the 'Left Turn' in Chartism which had two causal factors. The first was the eruptions of revolution across continental Europe in 1848 which reinvigorated the Chartist movement. Secondly, this was compacted into a short period of intense activity after the tactical error of Feargus O'Connor of not marching on Parliament with the Third Petition after a mass meeting on Kennington Green. It was delivered by hansom cabs instead and ignored. The state sensing weakness struck. This was relatively rapidly accompanied by Left papers coming to dominance edited as follows in London: The Democratic Review 1849-50, [ed] George Harney, The Red Republican & The Friend of The People 1850-51[ed] George Harney which contained in three editions the first English publication of Karl Marx and Frederick Engels The Communist Manifesto and Notes to the People 1851-2 [ed] Ernest Jones. The Communist Manifesto was translated by the Marxist-Feminist Helen Macfarlane. [72] Thomas Cooper, by this time, had become a deviationist moving rapidly rightwards embracing 'moral-force' Chartism. The latter reflected his metamorphosis from autodidact to professional writer and eventual reconversion to Evangelical Christianity. I shall employ primary texts of poetry from a 'Left' journal and Mathew Arnold. Also see continuity with Marxian socialism, beginning in 1843 with Engels and continuing with the shift toward internationalism in the circumstances of post-1848 Chartism, through the creation of the First International until the present. Thus, agreed with the orientation of Mark O'Brien's revolutionary socialist analysis. [73]

I shall employ a contrast to illustrate the polarized nature of society and thought when the adornments of ideology are torn away. Although there are graduations when that 'knock on the door' of history I mentioned earlier finally comes there are only two camps: exploiter and exploited. This will be illustrated by way of a poem written by Mathew Arnold: 'Dover Beach' and Leon Trotsky's meditation on Chartism. Firstly, Trotsky summing-up the Chartist experience:

> *The period of Chartism is immortal because over the course of its existence it affords us an abbreviated and systematic view of virtually the entire course of proletarian struggle...*

Now in contrast let us examine Arnold's 'Dover Beach':

...the world, which seems

---

[72] *on Trotsky on Britain* (New York, Pathfinder, 2012), p. 151.
[73] O'Brien, Mark *'Perish the Privileged Orders', A Socialist History of The Chartist Movement,* (London, Redwords, 1995.)

To lie before us like a land of
dreams, So various, so beautiful, so
new,
Hath really neither joy, nor love, nor
light, Nor certitude, nor peace, nor help
for pain; And we are here as on a
darkling plain,
Swept with confused alarms of struggle and flight,
Where ignorant armies clash by night.[74]

We see contrasting Weltanschauung or 'world-views. One, Marxian which understands the inevitability and progressive nature of 'proletarian struggle' and sees it ultimately leading to a new dialectical leap, 'the negation of the negation' and a higher level of socio-cultural development. The other comprehends a bourgeois 'new' world i.e. the establishment of capitalism as the dominant social system. However, Arnold's addressee is left in doubt as the 'speaker ejaculates three 'end-rhymes' 'pain'/ 'flight'/ 'night'. The masses are as always from the pens of rightist bourgeois commentators quite simply 'ignorant'. But whom are these 'ignorant armies. Are they England and France as Francis O'Gorman suggested[75] *Of course as Arnold's speaker concurs. Or rather is Arnold alluding in the final line of the poem to the 'armies that clash by night', maybe within, the class armies. For as O'Gorman observes: 'the generalist terms of 'Dover Beach' refuses to ground itself exactly.' (O'Gorman, 2017, p.312). Ostensibly about a crisis of faith, it was probably drafted, as (O'Gorman 2017 p.312), makes clear in 1851 but was not published until 1867.*

Yet in another world this was also published in 1851 in *The Red Republican & the Friend of the People*. {Ed} Julian Harney.[76] It included Ernest Jones' 'prison poems or 'Sacred Hymns'[77].

       BY ERNEST JONES.
-     *(Written in the blood of their author, whilst*
       incarcerated in Tothill-fields' Prison.)

       No. 1. —HYMN FOR ASCENSION DAY.

Chorus.   *Freedom is risen!*
             Freedom is risen!
             Freedom is risen to-
             day!
Single voice.   *She burst from prison,*

---

[74] Daniel Karlin. [Ed] *The Penguin Book of Victorian Verse* (Penguin Classics) (p. 381). Penguin Books Ltd. Kindle Edition.

[75] Francis O'Gorman *Victorian Poetry: The Annotated Edition* (Oxford, Blackwell, 2017) p.312.

[76] Black, David *Helen Macfarlane* (New York, Lexington Books, 2004).

[77] Harney, G. Julian <u>The Red Republican & the Friend of the People.</u> London: Merlin Press [etc.], https://catalog.hathitrust.org/Record/012289057

	She burst from prison,
	She broke from her gaolers away!
Chorus.	*When was she*
	born? How was
	she nurst
	Where was her cradle laid?
Single voice.	*In want and scorn;*
	Reviled and curst;
	'Mid the ranks of toil and trade.
Chorus.	*And hath she*
	gone On her
	Holy morn,
	Nor staid for the long work-day?
Single voice.	*From heaven she came,*
	On earth to remain,
	And bide with her sons alway.
Chorus.	*Did she break the grave,*
	Our souls to save,
	And leave our bodies in hell?
Single voice.	*To save us alive,*
	If we will but strive,
	Body and soul as
	well.
Chorus.	*Then what must we*
	do To prove us true?
	And what is the law she gave?
Single voice.	*Never fulfil*
	A tyrant's will,
	Nor willingly live a
	slave.
Chorus.	*Then this we'll*
	do, To prove us
	true,
	And follow the law she gave:
	Never fulfil
	A tyrant's will,
	Nor willingly live a slave.

The addressee is almost enwrapped within this secular hymn, it is not one of praise or lamentation but of defiance. It was published just two weeks after the release of Jones from prison. We see alternating tercets rhymed aab between the speaker and The Chorus. The speaker had created an alternative ascension narrative with a revolutionary and proletarian goddess breaking free from the prison. The refrains from The Chorus are questionings and when they are given the new commandment:

Never fulfil

A tyrant's will,

Nor willingly live a slave.

Rather than the Christian 'to love your enemies' they sing in unison a sextet abbabb of solidarity. This is an example of what Margret A. Loose called 'The Chartist Imaginary' which she defined as being: 'The political and the literary, for Chartism, were inexorable.' [78]

The failure of Chartism is correctly, in my view, diagnosed by O'Brien as a failure of a vacillating leadership. [79] *A failure of revolution in England, at that time claimed Marx, would make any revolution 'in Europe a storm in a teacup.'* [80] *However, O'Brien's position is contested by one of the leading scholars of Chartism, John Saville in his 1848 The British State and the Chartist movement* [81]. *In particular the schema for the failure of 1848 to transmute into a revolutionary situation is contested. O'Brien does not cast aspersions on Feargus O'Connor's character or bravery. He made an error, as did others in the leadership. However, if the 'the charter and something more' had succeeded. That would have been, by my analysis, a circumstance which would have provided the material base for the triumph of a British proletarian poetics and also a massive boost to the international worker's movement. Saville argued two clear lines in his explanation for this catastrophe: To understand Chartism in 1848 we should:*

> *'locate British domestic politics within the triangle*
> *of revolutionary Paris, insurgent Ireland, a revitalized*
> *Chartist movement in London and the industrial North.'*
> [82]

I do not think many Marxists would disagree with him there. However, he continues that once the tide had ebbed in France and Ireland the Chartists were lost. No, that is to see it camera obscura for as Marx had argued above, England was the key to a successful continental revolution because of its higher development of Capital. Saville' second error is on the nature of revolution. While correctly criticizing those theoreticians, who saw the demise of the worker's movement as one of being granted gradual concessions by the bourgeoisie. [83] *He comprehends the coercive strength of the state apparatus as the concrete reason for the lack of a revolution. This meshes conveniently with his membership of the Communist Party of Great Britain who were*

---

[78] Loose, Margret A, *The Chartist Imaginary* (Ohio, Ohio State University, 2014), p.3

[79] O'Brien, (1995 pp.71-74).

[80] Marx, Karl '*On Poland*' Marx/Engels Collected Works Vol. 6, p.389.

[81] Savile, John 1848 *The British State and the Chartist movement (*Cambridge, Cambridge University Press 1990). *p.1*

[82] Saville (1990) p.1

[83] Barrington, Moore. Jr. Social Origins of Dictatorship and Democracy (Boston, Beacon Press, 1996) p.39.

advocating the parliamentary road to socialism in Britain at the time he was writing. Paradoxically there can be little doubt that in London in 1848 the ruling class thought revolution was in the air. The Duke of Wellington was called from retirement to lead the troops, 100,000 special constables were recruited from the ranks of the petty-bourgeoisie and the Royal Family were transferred to the Isle of Wight.

However, the masses did not simply retreat back to their hovels and cottages afterwards. As Heaney, wrote in 1850:

> *In the past those Chartists who espoused socialist programmes had been denounced as "utopian" and "dangerous". But time has brought them to two alternatives: a retreat from the Charter into 'bourgeois idealism' or the bordering of the agitation to include socialist aims*[84]

An essential aspect of my argument is that 'labour' when not estranged from itself is the creative and collective expression of humanity and when given propitious circumstances i.e. communism it will develop into myriad forms with infinite possibilities thus we can see the magnitude of the defeat of Chartism for labouring-class literature. I agree with Leon Trotsky that in the higher stages of communism:

> *The average human type will rise to the heights of an Aristotle, a Goethe, or a Marx. And above this ridge new peaks will rise.*[85]

So, I suggest, that when the masses are in a heightened state of class consciousness. When the proletariat is a 'class-for-itself' (Marx) and aware of itself as the 'subject' of history then their potential for creativity is increased. We saw this during Chartism with poetry and will observe it in the early years after the Russian October 1917 revolution. I shall examine some of the ideas around this aesthetic in the conclusion. Thus, I have shown how the genres employed by the labouring classes are, in the last instance, moulded by the level of class struggle.

---

[84] Schoen, A.R *The Chartist Challenge* (London, Heinemann, 1958) p 197
[85] Trotsky, Leon, *Literature and Revolution* (London, Redwords, 1991), p. 284.

Nigel Pearce

Finally, a poem by Gerald Massey.

THE MEN OF "FORTY-EIGHT."

They rose in Freedom's rare sunrise,
*   Like giants roused from wine!*
And in their hearts, and in their
*   eyes, The God leapt up divine!*
Their souls flashed out like naked swords,
*   Unsheathed for fiery fate;—*
Strength went like battle with their
*   words, The men of Forty-eight.*
Hurrah!
*   For the men of Forty-eight.*

Dark days have fall'n! yet in the
*   strife, They bate no more*
*   sublime,—*
And bravely works the fiery life,—
*   Their hearts' pulse thro' the*
*   time.*
As grass is greenest trodden down,
*   So suffering makes men*
*   great;*
And this dark tide shall grandly
*   crown The men of forty-eight.*
Hurrah!
*   For the men of Forty-eight.*

Some, in a bloody burial sleep,
*   Like Greeks, to glory*
*   gone!*
Swift in their steps, avengers leap
*   With their proof armour on!*
And hearts beat high with dauntless
*   trust, We'll triumph soon or late,*
Though they be mouldering in the
*   dust,— Brave men of Forty-eight.*
Hurrah!
*   For the men of Forty-eight!...*

[...}

Ye'll find them all elate,—
And true as ever Spartan band!
    The Men of Forty-eight.
Hurrah!
    For the Men of Forty-eight. [86]

Two things about Massey's poem strike the reader. Firstly, its verbose language to describe the zenith of working-class struggle in Britain, there is a dissonance between subject and form. And secondly, his convolution of secular and sacred registers. In Massey's case unlike Jones, this does represent a genuine confusion for as (Randle 1999, p.190) illustrates he vacillated between militant class poetry to be an apologist for British Imperialism. I argue that this was because having no systematic method he just reacted to events. Perhaps here we have the kernel of why the Bolsheviks created a situation where a revolution and therefore the material base for a proletarian poetics existed. Because Lenin affirmed 'without revolutionary theory, there can be no revolutionary practice.' The British working class by its very nature would have had 'combined and uneven consciousness.' This required not a loose network of newspapers publishing poetry. But a vanguard party with a full spectrum of publications both literary and political necessary if the Gramscian 'war of manoeuvre' was to be won which is the prerequisite for the victory of the social revolution. The latter being the requirement of a proletarian poetic.

---

[86] Massey, Gerald *The Poetical Works Complete in One Volume.* (Boston, Ticknor and Fields, 1857) p.103-104

49

Nigel Pearce

Conclusion.

V.I. Lenin focused on the problems of the writer under capitalism. He suggested:

> *One cannot live in society and be free from society. The freedom of the bourgeois writer, artist or actress is simply masked (or hypocritically masked dependence on the money-bag, on corruption...* [87]

Thus, as I suggested one must argue it is a consequence that for working-class writers, like the Chartists, to be free there must be a qualitatively different society.

> *The history of Chartist literature is not only a struggle for new subject matter but also a most complex search for a new literary method.* [88]

Therefore, I reiterate that a prerequisite for a proletarian poetic is the gaining of State power by the masses. Only then do the societal conditions exist to facilitate what Boris Arvatov called Life-Building. In this context Lenin continued his musing on the problems of literature:

> *(Ours) will be a free literature because of the idea of socialism and sympathy with the working people .* [89]

The aesthetics of William Morris could be understood as an attempt to remove the division of labour between the artist or indeed poet, and manual labour. An attempt to reintroduce some of the lessons he had learnt from John Ruskin but from the standpoint of Socialism and is understood as an advance. It is of significance to note that Trotsky thought the conditions were not ripe for Boris Arvatov concept of shiznestraitalststn (Life-building) which was the total decommodification and thus de-fetishization of the process of art and poetry as it would take place in the 'means of production'. Art would become indistinguishable from any other form of production. Boris Arvatov (2017 [1926, p.15) argued:

> *Art and life – how should these apparently heterogeneous phenomena be connected to each other?*
>
> *The question is a stumbling block in front of bourgeois science and bourgeois practice, unsolved and unsolvable in the conditions of capitalist society.*

Hence this school amongst many others who were debating art and literature in the early days of the revolution called themselves Productionists. With the ambitions of eradicating the artificial division of mental/physical labour. Or as Alexander Bogdanov wrote:

---

[87] Lenin, V.I *Collected Works Volume 10*, Moscow, Progress Publishers, 1965, p. 68.
[88] Kovalev Y.V *Victorian Studies* Vol. 2, No. 2 (December 1958) p.126.
[89] Lenin (1965), p.10,

To organize the forces in his social world, his struggle...the proletarian needs a new class art. The spirit of this art is the collectivisation of labour; it assimilates and reflects the world from the viewpoint of its feelings... its creative will... [90]

Bogdanov coined the term 'proletarian monism'. This is essential to understanding proletarian literature and art. Bogdanov thought 'collective labour' embraced every aspect of a human and embracing all 'elements of experience' and counterposed it to 'bourgeois dualism' where there is not this unity but division. As I mentioned Lenin was arguing against this as early as 1920 as did Trotsky in Literature and Revolution, 1924. More generally it was argued by both Lenin and Trotsky that because the class-conscious Russian proletariat had been decimated in three years of Civil War. Sixteen armies from Imperial powers fought on the side of the counter-revolutionaries. Although the revolution had been saved, but to quote Lenin in 1922 at a huge cost which was 'a worker's state without a working class.' This created the conditions which prefigured the Stalinist Gulags and Show Trials.
Ultimately including the eradication of the Central Committee who had ordered the October 1917 insurrection, except for Stalin, by 1940.

Boris Arvatov was on the far-Left of the aesthetics Renaissance, which briefly flowered in the U.S.S.R. with those in Prolecult. Their ideas, in my view, were largely correct, but the objective conditions ultimately did not allow their implementation. Where does this leave the proletarian poetic aesthetic, Marxism? I agree with the poet Vladimir Mayakovsky, who worked for the revolutionary Left Front for the Arts. It must endeavour:
> *[to] re-examine the ideology and practices of so-called leftist art, and to abandon individualism to increase art's value for developing communism."* [91]

My findings are therefore that, firstly there is a dialectical relationship between social class and poetry. Although this is complexified by the 'relatively automatous' nature of the base to the superstructure. An example of this would be Raymond Williams' important contribution 'Base and Superstructure.' [92] *We understand that they have a dialectical relation, interacting upon each other. I have shown a dialogue between Romanticism and early Chartist poetry noting the work of Janowitz (1998) and Sanders (2009). Also, I noted a change of genre and also a change in the percentage of the numbers of Chartist and non-Chartist poets submitting work after the defeat of the 1842 General Strike. This led to the backward looking O'Connoirite Land Scheme. Chartism and its poetics were revived in 1848 giving a glimpse of what a proletarian aesthetic could resemble. The only occasion that there existed a material base for a labouring class poetics, I suggested, was the brief period following the October 1917 revolution until the counter-revolutionary and*

---

[90] Bogdanov, Alexander The Proletariat and *Art* Bowlt [Ed] *Russian Art of the Avant-Garde* (London, Thames & Hudson 2017) pp 176-177

[91] https://monoskop.org/LEF

[92] Williams, Raymond. *Base and Superstructure in Marxist Cultural Theory"* New Left Review, no. 82, 1973, p. 3.

doctrinaire imposition of Socialist Realism upon the international workers' movement at the World Writers Congress in 1934. Once Stalin had proclaimed writers should be 'the engineers of the human soul.'[93]*The phrase occurred in conversation between Stalin and Maxim Gorky on October 26th, 1932. Mayakovsky would commit suicide rather than become a mouth- piece for Stalin and his new ruling class.*

I would suggest that an area of potential research would be a comparison of the writings of political prisoners during the Chartist period and those of Irish prisoners held as a result of 'The Troubles' 1969-1998. The primary sources for both exist. An analysis by genre, class composition and the relationship to the dominant poetics of each epoch may bear some interesting fruit when juxtaposed. One could imagine Ernest Jones and Bobby Sands as possible writers of both poetry and prose for comparison and analysis.[94]*Or equally the prison poems of Victor Serge in the Stalinist gulag in 1933 come to mind as a possible alternative. As well as his significant prose-fiction and other writings all available to the scholar. Although with Serge the question of translation would need to be answered. Also, of interest would be researching the largely neglected area of working-class women poets in the 19th century. I note the recent research of Florence Boos.*[95]

The movement of the oppressed in Britain has yet to gain the heights of the

Paris Commune, 1871 which Anne Janowitz references or that brief flowering in Russia 1917- 34 with its experiments in poetry and art. So finally, my analysis had considered two types of poetic. The Romantic which, although it employs the language of 'the ordinary people' is profoundly individualistic and the proletarian which is anti-individualistic but not against the individual. It is a multi-voiced collectivity. I did find an echo of Romanticism in proletarian verse; indeed, it was the dominant cord until the defeat of the 1842 General Strike in Britain. Again, hope arose renewed with the victory of the October revolution in Russia and a blooming of all the arts until it's defeats at the hands of the Stalinist bureaucracy. Yet today the world is in chaos and because the proletariat and its movements are the agency of social transformation. We must put our pens to paper to write poetry and organize in the tradition of Ernest Jones, Vladimir Mayakovsky and in the spirit of Chartism and the October Revolution.

---

[93] Stalin, *Collected Works*, vol.13 (Moscow, 1953) p.410.

[94] Serge, Victor *Resistance* (San Francisco, City Lights Books, 1989)

[95] Boos, Florence [ed] *Working-Class Women Poets In Victorian Britain* (Plymouth, Boordview Press, 2008).

Nigel Pearce

Bibliography.

Primary Sources.

Arnold, Mathew *Literature and Dogma preface.*

https://hdl.handle.net/2027/uiug.30112073726298

Byron, Lord *The Major Works* (Oxford, Oxford University Press, 2008). Cooper, Thomas *The Life of Thomas Cooper Written by Himself* (London, Hodder & Stoughton, 1873).
Cooper, Thomas *The Poetical Works of Thomas Cooper* (London, Hodder & Stoughton, 1877).
Cooper, Thomas *The Northern Star* (1841).

Engels, Friedrich *Dialectics of Nature* (Moscow, Progress Publishers, 1976). Engels, Friedrich *Socialism: Utopian or Scientific* (*London*, Bookmarks, 1993). Feuerbach, Ludwig *The Essence of Christianity*, George Eliot (Translator) (New York *Dover Philosophical Classics 2008).*

Frost, Thomas *Forty Years' Recollections: Literary and Political* (London: S. Low, Marston, Searle, and Rivington, 1880).
Gammage, R.C. *History of the chartist movement* (London, Merlin Press, (1976 [1894]).
Jones, Ernest *The Battle-Day and Other Poems* (London, Routledge & Co, 1855).
Jones, *The Labourer*,1846.

Jones, Ernest The Labourer vol 1, 1847.

Jones, Ernest (1847b) 'Literary Review', The Labourer, vol 2, 1847.
Harney, G. Julian The Red Republican & the Friend of the People. *London: Merlin*

Press [etc.], *https://catalog.hathitrust.org/Record/012289057*

Keats, John, *The Complete Poems* (London, Penguin Classics, 1973).

London Corresponding Society, Nov 19th, 1794 (1795).

Karl, Marx & Frederick, Engels, *Collected Works, 50 vols, vol 3 published or in preparation* (London, 1975-n/a).

Marx, Karl & Engels, Frederick *Collected Works in 50 vols*, vol 4 (New York, International Publishers, 2004).

Marx, Karl *Early Writings* (London, Pelican Marx Library,1977).

Marx, Karl & Engels Frederick *Literature and Art: Selections from Their Writings* (New York, International Publishers, 1947).

Marx, Karl & Frederick Engels On Britain (Moscow, Foreign Languages Publishing House, 1953).

Marx, Karl. & Frederick Engels *On Literature and Art* (Moscow, Progress Publishers, 1976).

Marx and Engels *On the Trade Unions* (New York, International Publishers, 1987).

Marx, Karl. & Frederick Engels *Selected Correspondence, 1846-1895 Marxist Library, 29, (*New York, International Publishers 1942).

Marx, Karl. & Frederick Engels *Selected Correspondence* (Moscow, Progress Publishers,*1965*).

Reminiscences of Marx and Engels (Moscow, Foreign Languages Publishing House, 1963).

Karl, Marx & Frederick Engels *The German Ideology* (London, Lawrence & Wishart,1982).

https://www.marxists.org/archive/marx/works/1852/18th-brumaire/ch01.htm

The Marx-Engels Correspondence, *The Personal Letters, 1844-1877*. (London, Weidenfeld and Nicolson, 1981).

Massey, Gerald *The Poetical Works in One Volume,* (Boston, Ticknor & Fields M CCC LVII).

Mill, John Stuart. "Thoughts on Poetry and Its Varieties." (The Crayon, vol. 7, no. 4, 1860).

Morris, William *Useful Work v, Useless Toil* (London, Penguin Books, Great Ideas, 2008).

Rousseau, Jean-Jacques. *On the Social Contract* (New York, Dover Thrift Editions, 2016).

Ruskin, John *Selected Writings* (Oxford, Oxford University Press, 2009). Shelley, Percy Bysshe, *The Major Works* (Oxford, Oxford University Press, 2003).

Tennyson, Alfred, *The Major Works* (Oxford, Oxford University Press, 2009).

The Chartist Circular, By permission of the British Library Board. *The Northern Star and the Leeds* General Advertiser British Library Newspapers & Periodicals: *http://find.galegroup.com.libezproxy.open.ac.uk/bncn/start.do?prodId=BNCN&u*

Wordsworth, William *Letters of William Wordsworth: a new selection* [Ed] Alan

G. Hill. (Oxford, Oxford University Press, 1984).

Wordsworth, William. *The letters of William and Dorothy Wordsworth: The later Years, 1821-1853* (2nd Ed.) (Vols. 1-4). (Oxford, Oxford University Press, 1978- 1988).

Wordsworth, William. *Wordsworth's Political Writings (Kindle Edition).* Wordsworth, William *The Major Works* (Oxford, Oxford University Press, 2000).

Secondary Sources.

Althusser, Louis *Lenin and Philosophy and other essays* (India, Akkar Books, 2006).

Allen, Joan and Ashton. A. Owen [ed] *Papers for The People A Study of the Chartist Press* (London, The Merlin Press, 2005).

Arvon, Henri *Marxist Esthetics* (London, Cornell Press, 1973).

Arvatov, Boris *Art & Production* (London, Pluto Press, 2017[1926]).

Barrington, Moore. Jr. *Social Origins of Dictatorship and Democracy* (Boston, Beacon Press, 1996).

Black, David *Helen Macfarlane* (New York, Lexington Books, 2004).

Blair, K & Mina, G [ed] *Class and Canon, Labouring-Class Poetry and Politics 1750-1900* (London, Palgrave Macmillan, 2013).

Benjamin, Walter *The Work of Art in the Age of Mechanical Reproduction*

(London, Penguin Great Ideas, 2008 [1936]).

Bogdanov, Alexander The Proletariat and Art *in* Bowlt [ed*] Russian Art of the Avant-Garde* (London, Thames & Hudson 2017).

Boos, Florence [ed] *Working-Class Women Poets In Victorian Britain*

(Plymouth, Boordview Press, 2008).

Bowlt, John E [ed]. *Russia Art of the Avant-Garde* (London, Thames & Hudson, 2017).

Brecht, Bertolt, in *Paulo Freire: A Critical Encounter (1993)* by Peter McLaren and Peter Leonard (London, Routledge, 1992).

Briggs, Asa Chartism (Stroud, Sutton Publishing,1998).

Caudwell, Christopher, *Illusion and Reality* (Lawrence & Wishart, 1973 [1937). Caudwell, Christopher *Culture as Politics* (Pluto Press, London, 2018).

Chandler, James K *Wordsworth's Second Nature: A Study in the Poetry and Politics* (Chicago, University of Chicago Press, 1984).

Chase, Malcolm *Chartism A New History* (Manchester, Manchester University Press, 2007).

Charlton, John *The Chartists: The First National Workers' Movement* (London: Pluto Press, 1997).

Cunningham, Valentine *Victorian Poets: A Critical Reader* (Oxford, Wiley Blackwell, 2014).

Eagleton, Terry *Literary Theory: An Introduction* (Oxford, Blackwell, 1996). Eagleton, Terry *Marxism and Literary Criticism* (London, Routledge Classics 2008),

Epstein, James *The Lion of Freedom* (London, Breviary Stuff Publications, 2015).

Foot, Paul, *The Vote (*London, Bookmarks, 2012).

Goodridge, John: https://lcpoets.wordpress.com/introtobibliography/

Goodway, David *London Chartism 1838-1848* (Cambridge, Cambridge University Press, 1982).

Goodway, David *George Julian Harney: The Chartists were Right.* (London, Merlin Press, 2015).

Gramsci, Antonio 'The Formation of Intellectuals' in *The Modern Prince and Other Writings (New York, International Publishers, 1978).*

Gramsci, Antonio *Selections from the Prison Notebooks.* (London, Lawrence and Wishart, 1982).

Groves, Reg *But we shall rise again: A narrative history of Chartism* (London, Secker and Warburg, 1938).

Karlin Daniel. [Ed] *The Penguin Book of Victorian Verse* (Penguin Classics), Penguin Books Ltd. Kindle Edition.

Kovalev, Y. *An anthology of Chartist Literature* (Moscow, Foreign Languages Publishing

House,1956).

Kovalev, Y. *Victorian Studies Vol. 2*, No. 2 (December 1958).

Krantz, Mark *The 1842 General Strike* (London, Bookmarks, 2014).

Krishnamurthy, Arura *The Working-Class Intellectual in Eighteenth-and Nineteenth-Century Britain* (London, Taylor & Francis, 2009).

Hall, Robert, G *Voices of the People,* (Wales, Merlin Press, 2007).

Hartmann, Geoffrey *Wordsworth Poetry 1787-1814* (London, Yale University Press, 1974).

Haywood, Ian [ed] *The Literature of Struggle: An Anthology of Chartist Fiction*

(London, Routledge, 1995).

Hemingway, Andrew *Marxism and the History of Art* (London, Pluto Press, 2006)

Janowitz, Anne *Lyric and Labour in the Romantic tradition*, (Cambridge, Cambridge University Press, 1998).

Jenkins, Mike *The General Strike of 1842* (London, Lawrence & Wishart, 1980).

Johnson, Pauline *Marxist Aesthetics*, (London, Routledge Revivals, 1984). Lenin, V.I *Collected Works Vol 10*, (Moscow, Progress Publishers, 1965). Lenin, V.I. *Collected Works Vol 30* (Moscow, Progress Publishers, 1965). Loose, Margaret. A *The Chartist Imaginary: Literary Form in Working-Class Political Theory and Practice*. (Ohio, Ohio State University Press, 2016).

Lukács György *History & Class Consciousness: Studies in Marxist Dialectics,*

(Pontypool, The Merlin Press, 2010).

Mahamdallie, Hassan '*Crossing the river of fire: the socialism of William Morris*

(London, Redwords, 2008).

Murphy. Paul, Thomas, *Towards a Working-Class Canon*, (Ohio, Ohio State University
Press, 1994).

O'Brien, Mark *'Perish the Privileged Orders', A Socialist History of The Chartist Movement,* (London, Redwords, 1995).

O'Gorman, Francis, *Victorian Poetry: The Annotated Edition* (Oxford, Blackwell, 2017)

Sanders, Mike *The Poetry of Chartism: Aesthetics, Politics, History*

(Cambridge,

Cambridge University Press, 2009).

Sands, Bobby *Writings from Prison* (Cork, Mercier Press, 1988).

Saville, John 1848 *The British State and the Chartist movement* (Cambridge, Cambridge University Press, 1990).

Saville, John *Ernest Jones Chartist* (London, Lawrence & Wishart, 1952). Scheckner, Peter *An Anthology of Chartist Poetry 1830s-1850s* (London, Associated University Press, 1989).

Schoen, A.R *The Chartist Challenge* (London, Heinemann, 1958).

Schwab, Ulrich *The poetry of the Chartist Movement: A Literary and Historical Study*
(Dordrecht, Kluwer Academic Publishers, 1987).

Serge, Victor *Resistance* (San Francisco, City Lights Books,
1989). Stalin, *Collected Works*, vol.13 (Moscow, 1953).
Stedman-Jones *Languages of Class: Studies in English Working-Class
History 1832-1982* (Cambridge, Cambridge University Press, 2008).
Rose, Johnathan, *The Intellectual Life of the Working Class* (London,
Yale University Press, 2001).
Randle, Tim Chartist Poetry and Song in *The Chartist Legacy* (United
Kingdom, Merlin Press, 1999).

Rennie, Simon *The Poetry of Ernest Jones: Myth, Song and the 'Mighty Mind'*

(London, Routledge, 2016).

Royle, Edward, Chartism (London, Longman, 1996).

Royle, Edward, *Revolutionary Britannia?* (Manchester, Manchester
University Press,
2000).

Taylor, Miles *Ernest* Jones, *Chartism and the Romance of Politics 1819-1869*

(Oxford,

Oxford University Press, 2003).

Trotsky, Leon, *Literature and Revolution* (London, Redwords,
1991). Trotsky, Leon, *Leon Trotsky On Britain* (New York,
Pathfinder, 2012).
Thompson, Dorothy, *The Chartists* (London, Breviary Stuff Publishers,
2013). Thompson, Dorothy *The Dignity of Chartism* (London, Verso,
2015).
Thompson, E.P, *The Making of the English Working Classes*
(Harmondsworth, Penguin, 1965).
Vicinus, Martha, *The Industrial Muse: A Study of Nineteenth Century Working-
Class Literatur*e (London, Croom Helm, 1974).

Williams, John *Wordsworth: romantic poetry and revolution*
(Manchester, Manchester University Press, 1989).
Williams, Raymond. *Base and Superstructure in Marxist Cultural
Theory* New Left Review, no. 82, 1973.
Williams, Raymond, *Culture and Society 1780-1950* (London, Vintage, 2017).

Nigel Pearce

The Evangelicals and Women in Community

How do differences in gender, class and age help define the nature of the Evangelical conversion experience and how far do some of the fictional characters of George Elliot and Hannah More illustrate the lived reality of the experience in late 18th and 19th century Britain?

Nigel Pearce

CONTENTS

Nigel Pearce

Aims of the Project and its Relationship to Course Issues and the Secondary Sources

This project attempts to create a coherent analysis of the relationship between elements such as gender, class and age in the context of the Evangelical conversion experience in late 18th and 19th century Britain. It will employ secondary sources, e.g. Luker, and the debate around Sunday Schools will be paramount. Fictional characters drawn from Hannah More and George Elliot[1] will embellish this project. Central to the question is the definition of Evangelicalism provided by Bebbington[2].

The paramount aim of the project is thematic in nature, i.e. the competing narratives such as gender, class and age creates a structure which is "relatively autonomous" in nature and in which we can examine and define conversionists experiences this structure is a complex model.

Firstly, this project will define a definition of conversionism[3]. This account of Evangelicalism, which provides a vivid account of the most extraordinary altered states of consciousness firstly in experience "wrestling with God" ("I saw Jesus hanging on the cross saying that your sins are forgiven") and finally "all guilt is gone and my soul was filled with unutterable peace"[4].

This delineation of a conversion experience contains a number of essential trends, the denial or wrestling with God, the direct and personal experience of

---

[1] Hannah More (1889), The History of Hester Wilmot, p123, George Elliot (1858), Scenes of Clerical Life, and George Elliot (1884), Adam Bede

[2] Bebbington, Evangelicalism in Modern Britain: A History from the 1730's to the 1980's, p5

[3] S Staniforth, Vol. 1 Wesley's Veterans, p5

[4] ibid, p5

crucicentrism and the purging of sins. "My soul was filled unutterable peace"[5]. This narrative of "agony and immense relief"[6] was archetypal in nature.

I am aware that preaching the gospel was a paramount method of converting individuals. The significance of conversionism was at its most salient when it was defined as marking the boundary between a "Christian and a pagan"[7]. However there was debate about the means of converting sinners Jonathan Edwards "believed in insisting on the reality of hell" (quoted in Bebbington)[8]. Methodism produced preachers who argued that "backsliders - the devil would soon toss them about in flames of hell with a pitchfork". The antithesis of Edwards was that "more emphasis should be laid on the forgiving love of God"[9]. So we have seen an essential conversion experience and it's consequences in creating cultural discourse and producing opposing tactics employed to convert, i.e. either hell or love. Intellectual debate with regard to the spiritual nature of conversionism was located within the Reformation. The Evangelicals argued against Catholicism and agreed with Luther that humanity is blemished by sin and that consequently even good works cannot be a path to salvation. It is only through justification by faith, i.e. by God's intervention rather than humanity's attempts at achieving salvation, that true redemption is achieved. However, within the Protestant tradition two models of conversionism are contested. Firstly there is the intense spiritual experience described by Stanford which is more proletarian in nature and secondly there is the

---

[5] Wesley's Veterans, p5
[6] Bebbington's Evangelicalism in Modern Britain: A History from the 1730's to the 1980's
[7] ibid, p5
[8] ibid, p5
[9] ibid, p6

gradualist approach of the Anglican Evangelicals. A leading theologian of this position stated "We require nothing sudden"[10].

As the 19th century developed, Evangelicalism became increasingly linked to bourgeois values. Examples of these developing links between Evangelicalism and bourgeois values can be seen by the growth of philanthropy and missionary work especially by middle class women. It is significant to perceive that the proletarian Early Methodism did not, in response, decline, but played an active role in dissent, e.g. Peterloo Massacre 1819. Finally, in this exploration of conversionism is a radical statement of a leading Baptist minister who in 1830 wrote "The sinner has powers to repent without the spirit"[11]. He later redefined his position. However nine students of Glasgow Congregational Theologists Academy were expelled in 1844 for self-conversionalism[12]. There would seem to have been a trend towards eliminated the elements of mystery from the conversion experience.

Differences in gender, class and age are all of significance in the process of defining and illuminating the complex nature of conversionism as can be seen from the secondary sources such as Halévy, Thompson, and Luker. This section is orientated to conversion experiences in the context of class. Halévy provides the foundation for assessing the social class nature of Evangelical conversionism.

He questions why wasn't there a revolution in 18th to 19th century England. He constructs a structure for this analysis and its elements, e.g. class, which is developed in the context of Methodism. Thompson develops and deepens Halévy's analysis.[13] Halévy's position is as follows "the elite of the working class in being

---

[10] Simeon on the New Birth
[11] Bebbington, Evangelicalism in Modern Britain: A History from the 1730's to the 1980's, p8
[12] ibid, p8
[13] Thompson, The Making of the English Working Class

viewed by Evangelical movement with the spirit for which the established order had nothing to fear"[14]. Hence class is essential to Evangelicalism. Conversionism was noted elsewhere because a converted worker would "work hard save money and assist his neighbour"[15]. Converted workers "solve the social problem"[16]. Sunday worship Thompson argued provided a sublimated sexual expression (Psychological Masturbation, Thompson) and it also provided the method of expressional repressed emotions[17]. These elements are paramount in understanding Evangelicalism as a process creating equilibrium under capitalism.

We have seen above and will see below the Thompson's model is contested, e.g. by Bebbington and Laqueur[18]. Thompson continues by addressing the pertinent questions put forward by Halévy. He argues that between the years 1790 to 1830 the direct indoctrination was of paramount significance especially with regard to Sunday Schools, with regard to proletarian experiences within Evangelicalism and to the centrality of conversionism. I will discuss first direct indoctrination, and second Methodist sense of community[19]. First the direct indoctrination can be examined in the context of Sunday Schools. An example of "religious terrorism" is apparent in Isaac Watts' "Divine Songs for Children" "There is not a sin that we commit nor wicked word we say that in thy dreadful book 'tis writ against the Judgement Day[20]. The abuse of children is apparent. It appears to be clear that Sunday School played a role in socialising children into passive and supine adulthood and that conversion experiences may, for example, emanate from a fear of God, as opposed to a love of

---

[14] Halévy 1906, The Birth of Methodism in England
[15] Bebbington Evangelicalism in Modern Britain: A History from the 1730's to the 1980's, p5
[16] N. G. During, Samuel Chadwick
[17] Quoted in Study Guide, p25
[18] Laqueur (1976), Religion and Respectability Sunday School and Working Class Culture
[19] ibid
[20] Watts, Diving Songs of Children, E. P. Thompson: The chiliasm of despair, off prints, p142 (A425)

God. Their spirituality may be debilitated for life. A competing analysis of the socio-cultural nature of the roles of Sunday Schools is provided by Laqueur[21]. He argues that Sunday Schools were institutions which employed mainly proletarian people and that they weaved a working class culture moulded by religion which was autonomous from the bourgeoisie, hence challenging the dominant ideology thesis. It is significant that over 2 million children[22] were sent to Sunday Schools. The question of Sunday Schools then centres on whether they were a) a place of religious terrorism or b) a relatively working class haven with inherently working class culture spirituality.

This dialectic is complex and multi-dimensional. It explores spirituality and the foundations of conversions in the context of fear of hell. However, what Evangelicalism can be seen by that class as inherent for independent working class socio-cultural refuge, and hence working class conversion experiences. Thompson also examines the Methodist community in relationship to the bourgeoisie and proletariat. Thompson argues that it is a community which was too euphoric[23]. But the open chapel doors "did offer to abandoned people the Industrial Revolution some kind of community."[24] Also Evangelicalism was not bound by the state and flourished in small discrete communities, e.g. tin mining[25], where "Revivalism in the limited localised sense of a sudden and spontaneous outburst of religious frenzy was experienced[26]. "These physical and psychic expressions, shrieks and the tear induced trances"[27] were examples of conversion experiences at their most florid. In

---

[21] Laqueur (1976),Religion and Respectability, Sunday School and Working Class Culture
[22] 1851 Religious Census quoted in A425 Study Guide, p75
[23] Thompson (1968), The Making of the English Working Class, p143
[24] ibid
[25] Luker (1980) Revivalism in theory and practice: The Case of Cornish Methodism
[26] ibid
[27] ibid

1851 "an estimated 43.8%" population of the country attended chapels on the day of the religious census[28]. Many experiences were condemned by the Weslyan authorities, who feared they evoked social discontent and popular protests. Hence we see the working class resistance ideology[29]. A minister, W J Warner, wrote that "as a result of great revivals in the past, the town, Penzance, swarms with backsliders, consequently popular revivalism could be the premise of a shallow and temporary conversion experience."[30] Hence there could be articulated a model "at times of depression the miners turn to riot rather than religion"[31] but may also experience hysterical conversion experiences and also at times of crisis seek solace in the chapel. Hence Luker illuminates a complex model connecting conversionism of class and chapel. He presents a tension between working class resistance ideology and which enabled it to support atrophied chapels based on volatile conversion experiences.

This theoretical case is examined as working class conversion experiences, e.g. by Thompson and Luker, we are left with a multi-dimensional model which ranges from "psychic masturbation", "religious terrorism", "the solace of the chapel", thus creating a positive conversionism and how conversion experiences could also be shallow.

This project is based on the following primary sources: George Elliot's, Scenes of Clerical Life and Adam Bede, and Hannah More's, The History of Hester Wilmot. These primary sources will be examined and then tested against the secondary sources discussed above. However, in order to ascertain what is necessary for historical enquiry the sources need to be examined in the context of

---

[28] ibid
[29] ibid
[30] Warner, The Wesleyan Movement in the Industrial Revolution, off prints, p35 (A425)

the writer's intellectual terrain. These themes, i.e. intellectual, spiritual and emotional, and the context of gender will define and illustrate Evangelical conversion experiences. This project will be primarily emanating from a gender perspective encapsulated as follows "the Victorian intense preoccupation with religious matters can only be compared to our own preoccupation with sexuality"[32]. Are these supposed opposites really "psychic masturbation"[33] in both 19th and 20th centuries. Here we can perceive the relationship between religion and sexuality, which feeds into conversion experiences.

A brief outline of Elliot's life will allow us to perceive her in the ethos in which she developed. The first for our purpose was her conversional experiences. However, as she read vociferously doubts began to erode her Evangelical faith in the Bible, divinely inspired became to Elliot a transition from faith to belief, i.e. she came to believe the Bible was a cultural item. She moved with her father to Coventry, and made the acquaintance of the local intellectuals[34]. They introduced her to Hennell's "An Inquiry into the Origins of Christianity". The Bible, Hennell argued was "essentially mythological writing"[35]. As a consequence of this process Elliot refrained from attending church. Elliot's intellectual development was rapid. The concept of realism addressed by Elliot is an attack on the "quality of romanticism" with its "rustic idles". "We have to be taught to feel or not be partisan of a sentimental peasant but for a peasant in all his coarse apathy and the artisan in all his suspicious selfishness"[36]. She also wrote "Art is the nearest thing to life, it is a

---

[31] Luker (1980), Revivalism in Theory and Practice: The Case of the Cornish Methodism
[32] David Lodge Introduction to 'Scenes from Clerical Life' p7
[33] Thompson (1968) The Making of the English Working Class
[34] Introduction from 'Scenes from Clerical Life', p13
[35] Hennell (1830) An Inquiry into the Origins of Christianity
[36] Essays of George Elliot (1968) ed. Pinney, Introduction, p15

mode of amplifying experiences extending our contact with our fellow men, beyond the bounds of our personal lot"[37]. Elliot's Scenes of Clerical Life replaces both Evangelicalism and false romanticism with realism which possessed both an aesthetic and a moral element. Elliot applies this realism to her characters and their introduction, e.g. the relationship of Janet Dempster and Mr Tryan is beyond caricature and moves beyond the "bounds of our personal life"[38]. Elliot delineates her method saying "I undertake to exhibit nothing as it should be; I only try to exhibit some things as they have been or are, seen through such a medium as my own nature gives me"[39], "A metaphorical vehicle of humanist values"[40].

We shall continue our examination of conversionism, firstly with middle class gender issues and their relationship to defining Evangelicalism. The project will draw themes from 'Janet's Repentance' in "Scenes of Clerical Life". Elliot has created a model of conversionism in Janet's Repentance. She is married to a drunken violent man. In order to cope with this benighted state she herself seeks solace in alcohol. However, Janet continues to carry out good works. We can perceive a middle class woman, while experiencing inner tempest, fulfilling her role as a philanthropist and the Evangelical preacher who ultimately becomes Janet's mentor and companion. Elliot is exhibiting the collision and the drama as not at all between bigoted churchmanship and Evangelicalism, but between irreligion and religion. Religion in this case happens to be represented by Evangelicalism[41]. For Elliot her "doctrine of sympathy" influenced by Feuerbach's 'The Essence of Christianity'[42] "Out of that heart out of the inward impulse to live and to die for man" creates a humanist model.

---

[37] Elliot (1848) Scenes from Clerical Life, p170-171
[38] ibid
[39] George Elliot letters
[40] Elliot, An introduction David Lodge, p8
[41] The George Elliot Letters ed. J S Haight, p347
[42] Feuerbach, The Essence of Christianity, Chapter 5, p3

So Janet's agony can be presented as a reaction to her husband's own poverty of the "original humanity"[43]. Hence we can understand religion being as a metaphor of humanism.

The process of Janet's conversion was articulated first from the ruin of alcohol and finally Janet's ejection from her own home. "Robert has turned me out. I have been in the cold a long while"[44]. She feels that she has no faith, no love left. The pivotal moment to Janet is when Mr Tryan "converts" by confiding his own sinful past. This expression of his hidden solidarity is clear with her. For Elliot Tryan's commitment to Evangelicalism is secondary to his humanity. Here we see our fellow men beyond the bounds of our own personal lot[45]. The metaphor for Elliot's scepticism to reconciliation in scenes with regard to her orientation to Christianity is "a sacred kiss" between hero and heroine, which concludes Scenes of Clerical Life. Hence religion is "perceived in a secular dimension".

This project will now examine Elliot's Adam Bede. It is a qualitatively different in that it is a story of working class characters, e.g. Dinah Morris, "they tell me is as poor as ever she was, works at a mill and "has much to do to keep herself"[46]. Her sermons can be contrasted with Mr Tryan's less ebullient expression. However, Dinah Morris also perceived a gentle cradling dimension of herself. She can be described in this statement "our moral progress may be measured by the degree in which we sympathise with individual suffering and individual joy"[47]. Also "sympathy", the one poor word which includes all our best insight and all our best love from pain

---

[43] Scenes from Clerical Life Introduction, David Lodge
[44] Scenes from Clerical Life, p340
[45] Essays of George Elliot ed. Pinney, p170-171
[46] Elliot, Adam Bede (1889), p63
[47] Elliott, Letter 15th November 1875

"I wouldn't mind if you'd stay and sleep here" and to her magnanimity "fetch Adam's new Bible with pictures in and she shall read us a chapter, I like them words in the Bible". Dinah and Seth were both innately offering thanks for the greater quietness of spirit that had come down over Lizbeth. This is what Dinah had been trying to bring about though all her still sympathy and abstinence from exaltation[53].

A graphic contrast is apparent here from the agonies of hell to the soothing compassion of sacred secular love we are made aware of the complex nature of Evangelicalism and it can present itself as dialectical. There are contradictions within its totality thus the conflicting poles, i.e. fire and love achieves a need for a synthesis, a totality of Evangelicalism which can reconcile its opposites in a synthesis which can be understood to reside with Dinah. Hence the apparent paradox is resolved. Fire and love are reconciled in a working class woman preacher.

Now we shall examine the primary source, The History of Hester Wilmot[54]. This perspective will be contrasted with two secondary sources, i.e. Laqueur (1976) Religion and Respectability in Sunday Schools and Working Class Culture. More's tract can best be seen as an Evangelical didactic tract however, its lack of characterisation is stereotypically combined with a simplistic plot. Essentially it is propaganda directed at the proletariat. We will briefly delineate the development of the tract. Rebecca, Hester's mother had a violent, uncontrollable temper. She was fastidious with regard to domestic chores. Her behaviour was such that John, her husband, having no corner to run to, took to the ale house so that which was at first

---

[53] ibid, p114
[54] Hannah More (1834) The History of Hester Wilmot, p127

a refuge too soon became a pleasure. As the dark, dire domestic situation declined he became lost in self-indulgence. Mrs Jones opened a Sunday School. Perceiving that none of the Wilmots attended she visited. Mrs Jones maintained that she would "teach her to fear God". Rebecca's reply was "I would rather you would teach her to fear me and to keep my house clean". Hester Wilmot attended Sunday School regularly. Her desire for learning, was such that she would work early and late to give her a little time to read her Bible. A reading of the Bible and Catechism were the source of comfort for her. Hester, as a consequence of her reading, became aware of her sins. "We are by nature born to sin". But she soon found the spiritual grace by which we have a new birth and gained righteousness[55]. We have comprehended the spiritual metamorphosis of Hester Wilmot.

Now I am going on to the ideological role of Sunday Schools. "When children are bad, comfort yourself with thinking how much worse they would have been but for you and indeed what a burden they would come to society". This is an example of Sunday School as a dominant ideology thesis. However it is abundantly clear that some would seek solace in the working class culture. Again we are presented with the contradiction but unlike the dialectic described above, this cannot be resolved.

The dramatic conversion of Mr and Mrs Wilmot can be summarised here. Hester's religion caused conflict between Hester and her mother. Mrs Wilmot developed a dangerous fever, Hester denied herself and nursed her mother. When John by gambling, lost borrowed money from Hester, which she had saved for her gown, he "stammered out a broken excuse he had lost the money". Hester forgives her father and John walked away mournfully and said to himself surely there must be something in religion since it exhibits a change of heart. He pondered the change in

---

[55] Hannah More, The History of Hester Wilmot, p123

Hester from a pert girl to as mild as a lamb, from vain girl to one contented with rags. When after a family tempest, John hears Hester pray for her parents, he fell down on his knees, embraced his child and begged her to teach him how to pray. Rebecca also experienced a conversion. "She knelt down by her husband and joined in prayer with much fervour". It is self apparent that More's work is mundane and banal and is composed as an instrument of propaganda. The difference in age between Hester and self evidently her parents can be perceived as significant to Evangelical conversion and how it can be defined. Age and Evangelical conversion is of interest here.

This thesis will now examine three moments in Hetty's life, in Adam Bede. Firstly, "Hetty's dreams of all of luxuries, to sit on a path in pallor, to have some large beautiful earrings such as they were all the fashion"[56]. Hetty is perceived as superficial and her dreams were not of meanings beyond her desire for trinkets. Her emotional life after reading Arthur Donnithorne's letter were shallow "all the girlish passion and vanity that made up her love"[57]. So here we conclude the first episode of Hetty's journey. The second episode is structured around Arthur Donnithorne's seduction of Hetty, his departure from military duty and Hetty's pregnancy, hoping as promised that Arthur would help her. In distress she begins her journey in search of him. "Poor wandering Hetty, with the roundish childish face and the hard unloving despairing soul looking out of it"[58]. The narrator considers "what will be the end, the end of this objectless wandering clinging to life only as a wounded brute clings to it"[59]. Elliot is creating another dimension here for, as a parallel to Hetty's wanderings

---

[56] Elliot, Adam Bede (1859), p100
[57] ibid, p335
[58] ibid, p391
[59] ibid, p391

in the objective material world, is another journey, a journey through her psyche, sometimes conscious sometimes unconscious. This is an interaction between her physical wandering which is pitiful and her dark abyss, this is a metaphor of archetypal magnitude. Hetty is arrested and found guilty of infanticide. Dinah enters the condemned cell. We are again presented with a metaphor of light and dark, day and night. Dinah holds Hetty "It was the human contact she'd come to but she was non the less sinking into the dark self. Dinah entreats Hetty to believe in a loving God who will forgive. If God our Father was your friend, was willing to save you from sin and suffering so as you would neither know wicked feelings nor pain again"[60]. Hetty does not respond and Dinah continues to encourage Hetty to "open your heart". There is a cordial relationship between Hetty's desire for secular comfort. "You won't leave me Dinah will you? You'll hang close to me". And Dinah's desire for spiritual salvation, Dinah perseveres. Dinah persuades Hetty to kneel "Dinah help me I can't feel anything like you, my heart is too hard."[61] Hetty confesses her crime to Dinah. Hetty clings round Dinah and shudders again. Elliot is ambiguous with regard to Hetty's conversion"[62]. What is apparent is that she experiences a cathartic experience and purgation. An experience of Hetty's conversion is not clear. It is possible to comprehend the dialogue in the condemned cell.

"One of human ruin, human love and the absolving process of two women sharing in the context of conversion, but the female caring defined as Evangelicalism as socio culture discourse provided a sense of emotional release. This can be illustrated in Elliot's 'Model of Secular Sympathy'. Nevertheless it is possible to perceive Hetty's experiences as spiritual for when Adam visited the condemned cell,

---

[60] ibid, 450
[61] ibid, p451
[62] ibid, p455

it is apparent that Hetty has had a conversion experience whether secular or spiritual. She experiences her own sins "I have been so wicked" and Dinah says "I shall forgive him, Arthur, else our God will not forgive me"[63].

Hence we are presented with two discourses. One which is defined as human and women's secular sympathy and two, spiritual redemption. These discourses are relatively autonomous and form a bi-dimensional model. The primary sources are orientated to women and Janet Dempster, Dinah Morris, Hester Wilmot and Hetty, they can be perceived as hetrogenic. "The Bible and domestic female mission", where women from different political and socio economic class, were 'co-workers'. However women's experience of Evangelicalism was different to that of men who had a more patriarchal perspective. Women however, "sought to regain Christ out of the heavenly Bible". The 1851 Religious Census was of immense significance for a society profoundly aware of religion. This was symptomatic of dissent in the proletariat and possibly popular unrest, e.g. Peterloo Massacre 1819 and the Chartists in the 1830's. Also the wave of revolution which swept Europe in 1848 created disquiet in the bourgeoisie. Popular unrest occurred but in localised fractions, as Luker describes in Cornwall. "At times of depression, the miners turned to riot rather than religion"[64]. Those who attended church were divided into a) rural - 71.4%, and b) urban - 49%. The apparent contradiction of tin miners rioting and the higher levels of church attendance in rural areas can be solved. Tin miners were not agricultural workers but industrial workers in a rural setting.

---

[63] ibid, p461
[64] Luker, Revivalism in Theory and Practice: The Case of Cornish Methodism

This analysis will construct an overview in order to provide a detailed analysis of socio economic class and social cultural matters within the context of the Evangelical conversion experience. It will become apparent that, not only did the Proletariat not attend church en masse, but the different strata of the working classes attended in different numbers, e.g. artisan made up to 23% of society, but 59% of Evangelicals non conformity. Unskilled workers made up an even smaller number of chapel attenders. Early Methodists in Lincolnshire 51% of lay preachers were agricultural labourers[65]. Developing this theme early Methodists, in the first part of the 19th century were composed as follows: 15% labourers, 20% miners, 43% artisans[66].

Here we come to perceive a connection with Halévy analysis "the elite of the working class is being embued by Evangelical movements with the spirit which in established order have nothing to fear"[67]. Hence it is apparent that the majority of the proletarians did not attend church "for adherence"[68]. Seth Bede is an example illuminating Halévy's thesis since, as an artisan and a Methodist he appears to be totally unaware of the class struggle that his class strata would lead, with a defeat to any particular unrest, e.g. the United Irish Rebellion (1789) led by Wolf Tone, who was a Protestant. A pattern can be perceived here when a political movement is perceived to be defeated "hope for improved conditions and political improvements in the present life". People responded by pinning their hopes or fears on the life to come. Thompson argued for an "Oscillation between political and religious excitement"[69]. As the latter increases the former subsided[70]. Mannheim articulates

---

[65] Obelkevich (1971) Religion and Rural Society: South Lindor 1825 - 1875
[66] Gilbert, Religion in Society, p63
[67] Halévy (1906) The Birth of Methodism in England
[68] Elliot (1854) Adam Bede
[69] Thompson, The Making of the English Working Class
[70] Study Guide p90

The theory of chiliasm "Chiliasm has always accompanied revolutionary outbursts and will give them rare spirit. When this spirit ebbs and deserts these movements, there remains behind in the world a naked mass frenzy and a dis-spiritualised fury"[71]. An example of chiliasm was the preaching of Joanna Southcott which flourished in the wake of the failure of British Jacobins and therefore the process of oscillation has swung from political to religion.

The rapid growth of Methodism during the wars was a component of the psychic process of counter revolution[72]. An example of this oscillation calls religion the hysterical conversion accompanying experiences is described by "a preacher of the Bible Christians". The conversion experiences were often accompanied by agonies, prostratorising and loud and pitying cries of penitence[73].

Socio-economic class and Methodism are symbiotic in nature. The most significant example of "spiritualised fury" were to be located in the movements which surround the major 'prophetess' Joanna Southcott. She preached her apocalyptic message to the masses "the lower class began to believe the seven seals are about to be opened[74]. Her apocalyptic fervour was closely akin to the fervours of early Methodism. It brought people to the point of hysterical intensity, the desire for personal salvation was intense. Again we can perceive a causal relationship between socio economic class and conversion experiences. The nature of the conversion experiences in the 18th and 19th centuries above is proletarian and we should expect this as a component element of the chiliasm of despair.

---

[71] Manheim (1960) Ideology and Utopia
[72] Thompson (1968) The Making of the English Working Class
[73] F W Bourge (1905) The Bible Christians
[74] Southey (1908) Letters from England

Having explored the working class, and their conversion experiences, this project will now examine middle class responses to conversionism and its consequence. An example from Scenes from Clerical Life (Elliot, 1858) is of interest. We shall explore Miss Rebecca Linnet. She possessed a sense of fashion which was transformed by the heroine of the novel which she was engaged with. However, "No-one could deny that Evangelism had brought a change for the better in Rebecca Linnet's person"[75]. A plain grey denim dress and plain white collar could never have belonged to her before that date. This is a change in her and expression which seems to shed a softened light over her person. Mr Tryan is not extreme but a "softened life". Rebecca Linnet, like many Methodist converts, was strengthened by the doctrine of assurance, and became involved in philanthropic work. Gender roles were addressed by Evangelicalism but as the 19th century progressed there was a decline in working class with preaches, e.g. Dinah Morris, and the rise in middle class philanthropy, e.g. Rebecca Linnet.

This project will now illustrate the question of age. The phrase "religious terrorism", is employed to illuminate the treatment of some children in Sunday School. The Commission on Mines interviewed a ten year old girl "If I died a good girl I would go to heaven and if I were bad I should have burned in brimstone and fire. They told me that at Sunday School and I did not know it before"[76]. This is an example of the relationship between age and Evangelicalism.

Another point about the relationship between age and Evangelicalism is that conversion was most common amongst teenagers[77]. Connected to this general observation is "the mean age of conversion among future Methodist ministers in the

---

[75] Elliot (1858) Scenes from Clerical Life, p268
[76] Cited in J L Hammond, Lord Shaftesbury, Quoted in A425 off prints, p142
[77] Bebbington, Evangelicalism in Modern Britain: A History from the 1730's to 1980's, p7

period 1780 to 1890 was 16.4 years. The mean age in the period 1841 to 1900 was 15.8[78]. An example of teenage conversion is delineated in the History of Hester More. She was 14 years old when she converted at Sunday School and succeeds in converting her parents so we have a spectrum of age from 10 years old to 16 years old. There is also the range of experience in Methodist ministers conversion in mid teens to the brutal indoctrination of a 10 year old girl at Sunday School. Although Hannah More can be perceived as propaganda, she carefully places Hester at the most fertile of age for conversion, 14. Teenage conversions can be explained by youthful idealism and following Thompson, an awakening in sexuality which was sublimated.

Briefly we will glance at assurance. Its roots lie in the conversion experience that normally accompany it. The foundation "has its roots in the inward persuasion that God was on their side"[79]. The doctrine of assurance provided a foundation of Evangelicalism.

Conclusion

Differences in gender, class and age helps define Evangelical conversion experiences. Firstly, we examined gender and class. The working class preacher Dinah can be seen as preaching the hell method of encouraging conversionism. But she also exhibits great compassion in nursing of Lizbeth Bede. She is in the tradition of the early Methodism and expressions of conversionism were intense and exhibited a more sublimated sexuality[80]. Elizabeth Linnet, who is a product of the developing gradualist tradition throughout the 19th century, provides an alternative "soft light". This is in stark contrast to the early Methodism. Mr Tryan is also in the

---

[78] ibid, p7
[79] Bebbington, Evangelicalism in Modern Britain: A History from the 1730's to the 1980's, p7

context, in that he expresses middle class gradualism, a stark contrast to the conversion experiences of Dinah Morris. We can perceive the demise of early Methodism and the rise of Anglican Evangelicalism during the 19th century. Middle class women became involved in philanthropic enterprises, e.g. Josephine Booth.

The question of age was addressed in relation to Evangelical experiences which were mainly teenage. This can be explained by youthful idealism and an emerging sexuality[81]. Conversion experiences have socio cultural expressions which can be perceived as a "chiliasm of despair" with a religious response to political defeat in terms of popular support, e.g. for Joanna Southcott. Therefore we can perceive those conversion experiences in the context of the defeats of the class struggle. However the method developed above suggests a complex socio cultural model which led to workers resistance ideology and the solace of the chapel.

---

[80] Thompson (1968) The Making of the English Working Class
[81] ibid

Bibliography

Primary Sources

A425 Study Guide

Elliot (1858), Scenes from Clerical Life

Elliot (1859), Adam Bede

Elliot, (1968) Essays of George Elliot, Ed. Pinney

Elliot, The George Elliot Letters

Hennell (1830), An Enquiry into the Origins of Christianity

Feuerbach (1844), The Essence of Christianity

More, Hannah, The History of Hester Wilmot

Southey, Letters from England

Watts, Divine Songs for Children

Secondary Sources

Bebbington, Evangelism in Modern Britain: A History from the 1730's to the 1980's

Bourge (1905), The Bible Christians

Bocock & Thompson, Religion and Ideology

During, Samuel Chadwick

Hammond, G. L. & Hammond, B., Lord Shaftesbury

Halévy (1906), The Birth of Methodism in England

Laqueur (1976), Religion and Respectability and Working Class Culture

Luker, Revivalism in Theory and Practice: The Case of Cornish Methodism
    in A425 Off Prints Collection

Mannheim (1960), Ideology and Utopia

Marx, Thesis on Feuerbach

Obelkevich (1971), Religion and Rural Society: South Lindor

Simeon, Quote "On the New Birth"

Smart, The Religious Experience of Mankind

Stanford, Wesley's Veterans

Thompson (1968), The Making of the English Working Class
    in A425 Off Prints Collection

Warner, The Wesleyan Movement in the Industrial Revolution

Poetry.

UNTITLED

(A haiku)

Moonbeams were jewels
In her hair, I was dazzled
Spellbound by lost love.

THE POET IN THE ASYLUM SAW PERFECTION OF FORM AND SOUL

I fall in love from time to time with a lunar roaming woman,
Who is like an ephemeral dust particle captured in a circle,
A knife is plunged and twisted in the tangled, knotted heart.

How many nails are driven in our hearts and spit in the eyes,
Until we recognise ourselves to be that hunched misanthrope,
Struck by love but then cursed from birth with bad blood.

Give them books, paper with pen to write so it will be alright,
Poets of broken glass, you cannot feign the authentic maiming,
If pens cannot assuage the hearts, increase their medication.

I prepare a fire with grace, the immolation of the word by fire.

A POET SAW PERFECTION OF FORM AND SOUL

He falls in love from time to time with the lunar ray woman,
Who is like an ephemeral dust particle captured in a circle
A knife is plunged and twisted into the tangled, knotted heart

Give him a book, paper with a pen to write, so it will be alright,
If pens cannot assuage his heart, increase a chemical cosh,
Prepare a pyre with grace, an immolation of the word by fire

How many nails are driven in our heart and spits in the eyes,
Until we recognise ourselves to be that hunched misanthrope,
Who fell in love, but had been cursed from birth by bad blood

Poets with hand mirrors you cannot fain maimed poets' pain.

ELEGY FOR ELISE COWEN (BEAT POET 1933-1962)

(Allen Ginsberg would refer to her as 'the intellectual mad woman' after her premature death. However, her work is now considered to be 'significant' in that genre)

Your smile is bright with magic it draws a verse,
To glimpse the straights whose vision is blurred,
Theirs is a gaze inert that is carried in a hearse,
But you who danced the naked poetics preferred

The peace of wombs, the warmth and the rush,
Our wasteland is frozen with promises, some kept,
This moth is wingless and burnt but come the dawn,
You are cupped in a wrinkled hand yet have written

A dirge of deserts whose biting sand sings your fix,
It lies enchanted upon the pages scribed in scribbles,
The sacred insanity has vibrated your soul, a matrix
For jewels tarnished by the whispered opiate kiss.

YBA0066A

A SOLITARY BECAME TRANSPARENT

She had shot a dream in her bruised arm,
It may not have touched her soft breasts,
Like dew on sandy desire was quenched,
No chaos now just one whispered name,
A forgotten lover floating one in a nebula.

But lips have turned from crimson to blue,
Pastel shades soothed stoned cold eyes,
Heaven was floating like Monet's lilac lilies,
A morphine angel swooped upon her body.

She seemed peaceful in the opiated reverie,
It had cast its spell on bloody solitary sheets,
No one knew who she was, quite transparent.

THE LABYRINTH

In this labyrinth of my mind there are shadows,
Walk through this maze with a light for defence,
You may wander into a dark zones, become lost.

A warren of passages, some lead to nowhere,
Others contain gossamer webs of lost dreams,
The Minotaur died from thirst, a fierce bull-man.

A fountain sustains me now with celestial stars,
This brook is pure, it can bleed a crimson gush,
That blood which bleeds from a wounded heart.

This labyrinth contains those flickering spirits,
Suicides kept safe here away from their hurt,
There are so many, when will you all wake up?

YBA0063A

MORPHINE OD

She shot a dream up a bruised arm,
Some lover touched her soft breast,
Like dew on sand, absorb her desire,
No chaos, just the gentlest whisper
Of forgotten names, but lips turned blue,
Pastel shades soothed stone eyes,
Heaven floated like Monet's lilac lilies,
The morphine angel stroked her mind.

She was peaceful, opiate reverie cast,
Its spell on her bloody, solitary sheets,
No one knew her age or place of birth.

www.ingramcontent.com/pod-product-compliance
Lightning Source LLC
Chambersburg PA
CBHW080845270326
41930CB00013B/3008